50 Real Ameri

A journey into the haunted history of the United States – 1800 to 1899

By MJ Wayland

Whenever I take up a newspaper, I seem to see Ghosts gliding between the lines. There must be Ghosts all the country over, as thick as the sand of the sea.... We are, one and all, so pitifully afraid of the light.
Henrik Ibsen, Ghosts.

Paperback originally published November 2013
This Version July 2023

ISBN - 9798854259170

Published by Sarkless Kitty

Author website
www.mjwayland.com

Artist website
https://unseely.com/

Dedicated to Louise

My guide to the biggest mystery in life,

Love.

Thank you for being my everything.

Contents

Foreword

Being a British-born ghost hunter, I have focused my attentions on the ghostly appearances within the United Kingdom. For the last twenty years I have explored archives and visited taken part in hundreds of ghost hunts and paranormal investigations – yet only a handful have taken place in the United States.

So why write a book about American hauntings?

Well, the basis of this book begins in 1980 when one Christmas day I received a copy of the "Usborne Guide to the Supernatural World". A highly illustrated book dedicated to "Vampires, Ghosts and Mysterious Powers" that set me on the path of ghost hunting. It was a strange book to a seven-year-old child. As much as I feared its contents, the more I read, the more I became scared, and the more I had to read on!

However, one day in January I reached page 100 and the beginning of the "Hauntings in America" chapter. The book detailed in a spectacular fashion the "Colorado Ghost Lights", the "Maryland Ghost Pirate" who appeared as a ball of fire and not forgetting "The Walsingham Ghosts" – a haunted house in which Horace Gunn witnessed a human head covered in blood floating over his bed. Well, that was it, the book was hidden for a year until I was of more of a non-nervous disposition.

But it was that fear that changed into curiosity. Here I am, still not able to look at page 104, and yet, researching ghost sightings in the United States. After completing "30 Real Christmas Ghost Stories" I decided not to write a book but to research some of the stories mentioned in that childhood book and this led to a twelve-month journey through America's newspaper and local archives.

Aside from uncovering some of the strangest ghost stories I have ever read, I have also discovered the following about American Ghosts:

- America's haunted history from a media perspective started in the 1830s, previous stories related to ghosts witnessed in Britain and not stories from the United States.

- The Bell Witch – This most infamous of ghostly cases from 1804 doesn't even warrant a mention in any newspapers from 1800 to 1890.

- Pre-1840s Americans were a highly skeptical bunch, more curious than believers. The Fox Sisters put paid to that, and the ghost phenomenon began to spread across the US and UK. The massive increase in "real life" reports of ghost activity in the media can be directly correlated with the first reports of activity at the Fox household.

- I discovered a few "classic" ghost stories were created by counterfeiters to discourage local interest in the areas they worked.

- By the end of the 19th century most of the United States' most famous mediums had been exposed as frauds or at least had several allegations against them. The Bangs sisters, Fox sisters and the Eddy brothers were all exposed to have faked seances and paranormal activity.

- The Capitol Building was without doubt the most haunted building in the whole of the US. And probably still is!

I am still researching America's hauntings and on doing so, I can see the change in the experiences that people were having from the 19th century into the 20th century. It is this change that I want to explore in a second book covering this time.

This first book I want to be a snapshot of the ghostly sightings reported during the 1800s but also one that provides an insight into the vast scale of alleged activity. So, we have the hoaxes, clairvoyants, and very way-out stories but we also gain a keen insight into the big stories of the day. The Robertson family, especially Clara became a local celebrity due to her experiences, the Hoffman family

6

had hundreds (if not thousands) of visitors travelling many miles to visit their haunted house and we have Mumler's Spirit Photographs that became a sensation in Boston and New York. All famous stories that I have brought to the fore.

The book also includes many stories that I have not seen in print before. I have tried to provide an eclectic selection so that the reader understands that a ghost sighting isn't a simple thing, it's a complex experience that even nearly two hundred years later we are trying to understand.

Whether you read from beginning to end, or choose a story at a time, delve, explore, and enjoy – these stories will perplex, confuse and no doubt send a shiver down your back.

MJ Wayland
York, England

Faces In the Windows

In 1871 and 1872, people in Ohio and San Francisco reported several unusual phenomena attributed to ghosts – could mysterious, faint human faces appearing in windowpanes really be spectral phenomena?

In May 1871, the Chicago Times reported that for months the cities of Milan and Sandusky, Ohio, were the focus of interest because images of human faces had appeared in several glass windows in various buildings. All the clippings from the newspaper archives report that the faces looked like an early type of photography known as daguerreotype – but slightly imperfect.

On inspecting the affected glass frames, the Chicago Times correspondent wrote,

> The first appearance of the glass is a stony steel color, interspersed with a dull ashen color. Or it has some appearance of water that has tar or crude oil mixed with it, and one can see the oily substance floating on the top of the water, giving it a variety of colors.

Does this suggest that it was actually some form of effect created by a hoaxer? The correspondent continued,

> When the discoloration of the glass is first noticed, there is no clearly defined outline of a human face, but gradually day by day, in the center of this discolored appearance, a face begins to shape and form, until it requires no stretch of the imagination to see the well-defined features of an individual who appears to be looking out of the window from the room within.

Strangely, if you entered the room to look at the face in the window, nothing could be seen. In several cases, the faces appeared on the windows of deserted houses, although there were a few that were occupied.

The plainest picture is that of a middle-aged man, upon the window of an old building in North Milan, across the Huron River. It was built for a hotel, and used for that purpose for a long time, but is falling into decay now, and is used as a dwelling house, and occupied by a Mr. Horner.

Deacon Ashley, a member in good standing in the Presbyterian Church, and a worthy man, keeps a jeweler's store on the south side of the square in Milan. One of these pictures commenced to show itself upon one of the upper windows of his store. The deacon protested, but day by day it continued to develop into the features of a black woman. The deacon called in the services of soap and sand, but that would not eradicate it, and finally, despairing of disposing it in any other way, he took paint and brush and hid it out of sight by painting the glass over, letting it remain so for a number of weeks, and then removing the paint from the glass, when he found that it was still there as plain as ever, and now he has come to the conclusion to let it alone, as he says it is growing plainer every day, so that one can see the ruffles around the border of the woman's cap.

The Exchange Hotel in Milan had two pictures; one resembled a Major Marsh who died soon after leaving the military. The other picture had three female figures who seemed to be holding a man in a reclining position, as if he had just died.

The town soon gained notoriety for the pictures and people from all over the country came to see the famous faces in the windows.

The New York Times also wrote about the faces, although with a more skeptical tone,

Scarcely in the memory of man have earthquakes been more general, tornados more frequent or fiercer, or floods more destructive. Never at any time have we had more wonderful seers prophesying evil to come. And, to complete our uneasiness, those unaccountable faces, which we had fondly

9

hoped were indigenous to the windowpanes of Milan, appear to be spreading themselves over the entire State of Ohio, and bid fair to convert every street in the country into a spectral art gallery.

Mr. E. W. Alexander wrote to the Sandusky Register that,

> On one window of a sawmill in North Fairfield, Huron County, Ohio, he has discovered no less than twelve of these pictures, representing every variety of sex, species, and condition of life. There are ancient philosophers and pretty women, there are horses and cats, and, as in Milan, there are many portraits of Washington in his old age. It is evident, therefore, that these ghostly photographers are at least patriotic, and that is some comfort."

However, I have discovered a further appearance of the ghostly faces – this time in San Francisco. Did a copycat hoaxer or the ghostly phenomena transfer to San Francisco in January 1872?

Situated between Lombard and Chestnut, 2119 Mason Street was a fine house; the small two-story building was the home of a French widow named Joergens. In September 1870 while on a visit to France her husband had died, and it was claimed that since his death everything had "gone badly with her."

At the beginning of 1872, several children had been playing on the street when they were alarmed to see a man's face looking out the window of the upper story. The widow ran upstairs but could see no face; however, when she ran outside, the face was clearly discernible.

Later that afternoon, Madame Joergens decided to examine the pane more closely and just to the right of the first face that appeared she could see the face and shoulders of another man, having the features of her deceased husband.

Joergens told newspapers that she was "loath to believe in the existence of anything supernatural and fearing that her eyes might have been mistaken she asked several friends who knew her husband to look at the pane." The "husband's" face gradually disappeared over the course of about three hours, but the other face remained.

The Bulletin newspaper reported,

> The face is that of a man in the prime of life, with dark wavy hair and whiskers. The view of the face is a full one; the head is resting on the left shoulder. The expression of the features is one of contemplative sorrow. In it a gentleman recognized the features of a French real estate agent, now alive and in this city, and mentioned this fact to Madame Joergens, who immediately stated that the person referred to was a relative of hers.

As with Deacon Ashley's glass pane, every effort was made to rid the pane of the face but with no success. Ammonia, vinegar, alcohol, and "every variety of abrasive matter had been used on the window," but still the face remained.

What could have caused these strange faces to appear in windows? Was it a clever hoax perpetrated by a frustrated photographer, or was it a defect in the panes that were mistaken for faces?

Sadly, none of the faces still exist to warrant further investigation, and we are left with a mystery that has perplexed the people of both Milan, Ohio, and San Francisco for more than a century.

The Haunted Bedstead

This is a story from an anonymous but prominent merchant and banker from Galveston, Texas, who related this story to a journalist in 1889:

In the seventies (1870s) some time, I became the proprietor of a hotel in a North Texas town, situated on the Houston and Texas Central. On taking possession of the establishment, I found that a new supply of furniture was needed so I ordered a number of bedroom sets from New Orleans. They were second-hand for the most part, but in most excellent repair.

One bedstead was really handsome, in a heavy, old-fashioned style, with much elaborate carving, and I was surprised to find that its cost was less than a third what I should have supposed it would be.

Inspecting this bedstead, I noticed that the headboard was stained by some darker spots, that seemed to be dried splashes of some thick liquid, and which I found impossible to remove by scrubbing, or to cover up with varnish. I placed this bedstead in a room known as No. 37. The first guest that occupied the room was a stalwart cattleman from near El Paso, with about as much imagination as a gatepost.

A little after he had retired, the night clerk and I heard a fearful yell from No. 37 and a fierce banging on the door which finally broke open and out fell the cattleman in his night clothes, trembling all over his big body as if in ague, and dripping with cold perspiration.

> "Look at the bed! Look at the bed!" he gasped. "Good lord! I'm afraid he's dead."

We ran to the bed, and finding it all right, concluded that he only had a nightmare, but he persisted that when he had put his lamp out there lay beside him on the bed a man with his throat cut and bleeding. In spite of the way we laughed at him, we found it impossible to get him to return to the bed, so I was obliged to give him another room.

A few nights after, a lady occupied No. 37, and as before, a scream was heard that rang through the house, coming evidently from that room. When the chambermaid went to Mrs. B's assistance, she found her utterly insensible. On being restored, she related the same story the cattleman had told, stating that when she got into the bed it was apparently empty, but on putting out the lamp the moonlight, streaming into the room, revealed the dim outlines of a man lying beside her, with his throat cut from ear to ear.

Hearing this, I began to grow alarmed for, to say the least, it was a curious coincidence that both people, unknown to each other, had the same dream. I requested the chambermaid to remain with the lady until she should fall asleep, but I had scarcely regained my own room before both women came running out into the hall, screaming in concert.

"I've seen it sir," cried the chambermaid, "and it's a ghost for I can swear it wasn't there when I put the light out."

Mrs. B said she had again seen the bloody specter when the servant extinguished the lamp that she might go to sleep sooner and insisted on going to the rival hotel.

I knew there was no hope of either of the women keeping their singular adventure to themselves and that if I did not wish my establishment to be ruined by reputation of being haunted I must at once find some practical, commonplace explanation of the circumstances. I still persuaded myself to believe that some shadow thrown by the canopy above or the headboard caused the delusion, so I resolved to occupy the room and bed on the following night.

First satisfying myself that there was no one concealed in the room to play a trick on me I lay down on the bed without removing my clothes, having a lamp beside me that I could lower to a thread of light or brighten to brilliancy as I chose. My eyes were attracted by the stains on the headboard, that to my heated imagination seemed singularly fresh, and so strong was the impression on me of they being still wet that I put out my hand to touch them, but was seized by such a sudden horror of the spots that I could not help drawing back. I got up and plunged my head into ice water, for I wished to particularly keep my brain cool. I mention this that you may all know that I was wide awake.

Getting back into bed, I lowered the lamp, and then glanced at the opposite side of the bed. My heart nearly jumped out of my mouth, for lying beside me, with his ghostly face turned full to mine, was a man, whose head was nearly severed from his body. The light of the full moon streamed in at the un-curtained, open window, and revealed the entire figure as plainly almost as the day could have done. His fixed, glassy eyes, glaring with unspeakable horror, seemed to gaze right into mine, and his outstretched, clenched hand to clutch at me. Every detail of his dress is clearly impressed on my mind, for I noted all in a kind of fascination. He wore a dark pair of pants, white shirt, then reeking with his life blood from that gaping wound in his throat and was in his stocking feet.

Sternly summoning all my courage and former skepticism, I turned up the lamp once more with my hand, while I kept my eyes fixed steadily on what I still told myself was a delusion wrought of moonshine, shadows, and imagination. Slowly as I turned the screw, and as the light grew brighter, the figure drew dimmer and fainter, until in the full glare the bed showed clean and empty. Passing my hand over the place where the phantom had lain, I satisfied myself that there was nothing tangible there.

I then gradually lowered the wick and watched the specter evolve once more from what I knew to be empty air. I was resolved not to accept such an experience on the strength of one sense alone, so conquering my horror of the object beside me, I put forth my hand and seized the ghost's arm. A chill so extreme as to fairly paralyze my hand, and to deprive it from all sense of touch, struck through me, and I knew I had been too bold in this attempting to solve a mystery unsolvable by man.

Human nature could stand it no longer, so, leaping from that fearful bed, I ran into the hall. Then I realized that it had been the courage and stimulation of sheer terror that had sustained me, for once out of the presence of that awful object I fell to the floor fainting and completed unnerved.

Next day that bed was made into kindling-wood, after I had these spots in the headboard examined under a microscope, which examination proved them to be blood.

I wrote to the police authorities in New Orleans giving a description of the dead man that I had seen and asking if anything was known of such a man, although I carefully refrained from any allusions to having seen a ghost.

I wrote to the house from which I had bought the furniture, but neither could tell me anything of the bed, or its phantom occupant. The bedstead had passed from hand to hand for years, never owned by any person longer than that person could help until it had been sold to me.

That is all I know of it, and though it leaves the whole circumstance shrouded in mystery, I cannot believe the man I saw had been most foully murdered and that his blood still cried for vengeance. To you who are still skeptical on the subject of the dead returning, I say; "If what I saw was not a ghost, what was it?"

The Ghost Clock of Boston

An unnamed quaint coastal town in Massachusetts, was once home to a strange phenomenon known as the "Ghost Clock."

In January 1899, the Boston Transcript investigated the home of Mrs. Pitman from Reed's Hill, who owned an old clock or at least the case of an old clock. In recent years, it had begun to tick. According to the Boston Transcript,

Even the most skeptical have been obliged to admit its existence and mysterious workings and to confess their inability to explain the power that controls it or to advance any reasonable theory upon the subject. It has been visited and examined by thousands during the past few years - by clergymen, scientists, and others of learning and experience - and they have all come away satisfied that there was no delusion or trickery in what they witnessed and filled with wonder at what they had seen and heard.

Could a simple clock case really astound scientists with its unusual phenomenon? The case was described as simply a wooden case of an "old fashioned clock," entirely destitute of works, and containing nothing but a coiled wire that once was a part of the inner workings. The original owner was Mrs. Pitman's father and to her recollection the clock had no pendulum or mechanism when it was in his ownership. For some reason, it was highly prized by her father and was always kept on the mantel of a seldom-occupied room on the second floor of the house. The Pitmans were church-going people and not known for being spiritualists or believing in the paranormal. However, one evening, quite clearly, Mrs. Pitman heard the clock strike clearly and distinctively - as if in perfect order.

When the strokes ceased, Mrs. Pitman turned to her father to express her surprise, when her father said, "It is striking for me; I am going away." She laughed in disbelief, but old man Pitman added, "I mean that I am going - never to return."

Strangely, and very suddenly, a few days later the old gentleman died.

Mrs. Pitman scarcely thought of her father's words until one day the clock began to tick as if it were in full working order. She called for her brother and together they stood silently, still listening to the monotonous "tick-tock" of the invisible pendulum with no explanation of what could cause the sounds. Unbelieving that it was a portent of death, like his late father claimed, or that somehow his father's ghost may be responsible for manipulating the clock, the brother contacted several clockmakers to investigate the sounds. After weeks of investigation, the clockmakers could not explain the strange ticking within the case.

Whether we are dealing with "real" contact with the dead in this case or not, Mrs. Pitman soon found that the clock would reply to questions that could be answered by a simple "Yes" or "No," and the responses were always sensible and accurate when predicting the future!

The house was now open to the visitors coming from far and wide to communicate with alleged spirits while asking the clock for answers. The Transcript reported,

> These answers would come not only for her own benefit, but for that of others as well, so that many have consulted it through her (Mrs. Pitman's) mediumship - if such it can be called - and always with satisfactory results. At times, when the visitors are musical, there will be heard a tinkling, as if invisible fingers were picking on the wire, and upon one occasion, there came to the astonished ears of a lady the opening notes of an air which had been the favorite of a recently deceased relative.

So, was the clock a communication device to the dead, or was it merely infested with deathwatch beetles - famed for making clicking noises, especially at night?

The Bride of a Ghost

If you walked past the home of the newlywed Browns in 1901, you would hear the sounds of a young couple madly in love. They were as happy as any young married couple could be and, from inside the house, you could hear talking and laughing. However, you would be mistaken if you thought the groom was alive.

Often billed as the "Strangest Romance Ever Known," Bessie Brown of Cameron, Oklahoma, the daughter of wealthy parents with a high social standing and said to be one of the most beautiful girls in Oklahoma, married the man she loved, or at least the ghost of the man.

"She is not demented. Her mind has been tested, her brain examined by specialists, and her actions have been watched carefully, and no trace of insanity can be discovered," printed the Chicago Inter-Ocean.

When interviewed, Bessie's father said,

> Bessie had been brooding continually over the death of John Allen, to whom she was engaged to be married when he was killed. We tried to console her in her grief, but she wanted us to leave her alone. We feared she would lose her mind if she did not stop grieving so intensely. I had a doctor visit her several times, and he said her mind was all right, but that she was failing in health on account of constant worry. That was a year ago. About six weeks ago Bessie brightened up so much we feared she was under the influence of some drug. Then one day she made the statement that she had seen the ghost of Mr. Allen, and that hereafter she would not be sorrowful anymore, for she was going to marry the ghost, and that now since his spirit had appeared to her, she must keep her promise.

> Mrs. Brown and I feared the poor girl had lost her mind surely by this time, so we sent her to Dallas for a specialist to

18

make another examination of her brain. He pronounced her mental condition perfectly normal and said that she was not under the influence of any drug. He said her case was a strange one, and that she must surely see the ghost she talked about so much. I asked her to introduce me to the ghost, and she said I could not see it, but it was with her always. She talked reasonably about it. She seemed to know that we thought her insane because of her strange declarations but insisted that she was actually going to marry the specter. She called upon our minister and asked him to perform the ceremony. He tried to persuade her that it was sinful that she should marry a mere apparition, but she insisted.

The minister went with Bessie last week into the graveyard where her lover was buried, and at midnight the ceremony was performed which united her to the ghost of the man whom she had promised to marry two years ago, but who was killed in a railroad wreck just a few weeks before the wedding. I believe after close study of the girl's actions that she truly thinks she is wedded to the ghost, and that the apparition appears to her as naturally as if the spirit were still in the body. We are trying to do everything we can to make her forget her ghost, but it seems as if we are going to fail.

Before the wedding, Miss Brown rented a pretty cottage and furnished it for her and her spectral husband. She was often seen sitting on the back porch conversing with her invisible companion or walking down the street in full discussion with her phantom husband. Being from such a good family, and knowing her to be a good Christian woman, many people believed in her marriage to the ghost of her dead lover.

The Jonah

Henry E. Archer was a proud railway man who spent twenty years in the service of the Illinois Central. In 1892, he discussed "Jonahs," cursed or haunted locomotives, with the St. Louis Globe Democrat:

> On Christmas Eve, 1900, a poor officer who lived in the Constable's Tower within the Tower of London, heard a long, drawn-out wail coming from the top of the tower. Since it was late, around 9:00 pm, he decided to investigate in case someone was breaking into the castle. When he reached the stairs, he once again the wail sounded but this time, closer.

> Suddenly he heard a distinct light footstep receding behind the arras (a wall hanging or tapestry) in one of the rooms down the corridor. In total, three times, a sad, low, wailing cry trembled through the tower, and each time the soft footfall was heard retreating behind the arras.

> The officer searched the whole tower several times, but nothing could be found. Days later, he met with Captain Jupp, a former guard at Constable Tower, and he confirmed that there had been similar strange activity reported by previous officers based there. Interestingly, Captain Jupp also claimed that several Chelsea Pensioners (retired ex-military) witnessed the spectre of a middle-aged gentleman of long ago with a peaked hat, pointed beard, cloak, and sword over Christmas.

> The ghost was seen walking with a dejected gait, his head sunk low and his hand to his chin; he was seen near the state apartments set aside as the governor's residence. In the state apartments, there have been rumors and conjecture that it is haunted and said to have secret passages running to and from the precinct.

Three Stories of Hauntings

Lippincott's Monthy Magazine was a popular periodical that ran from 1868 to 1915. It published original works from authors such as Conan Doyle and Oscar Wilde, as well as reports from journalists across the United States. Most issues contained references and reports to ghosts or paranormal activity across the United States. The following three stories I have selected for their unusual strangeness.

Sometimes as a paranormal historian, one discovers very strange stories that seem so unusual that surely, they must be true? Well, I will leave it to you to make the decision on these tales of American weirdness from 1884:

Approaching Death

In Linn County, of the State of Iowa, there lived about forty years ago (1844) a well to do farmer, whom we will call Mr. G. He was a Pennsylvanian by birth but had married and reared a large family in Ohio, and when he emigrated to Iowa in about 1834 the only child remaining at home was a daughter born to the farmer and his wife late in life, and just entering her teens when they moved to what was the "Far West." At the time of this occurrence, I am about to relate, this daughter, who was my informant, was about eighteen years of age.

One evening in the early summer the men and maids had gathered to milk the cows. The farmer stood nearby feeding the pigs and the daughter was helping the maids. Contrary to the usual custom, the cows had not been driven into their yard, but stood outside and near the public road, which was not, however, in those times much frequented.

Suddenly a noise, as of a heavy wagon furiously driven, broke upon the stillness, coming nearer and nearer, until the clattering of the horses' hoofs and the rattling of the wheels could be distinctly heard. Mr. G called out to the milkers,

"You had better get out of the road; I expect a runaway is coming" and with that all withdrew to one side, though as yet nothing was to be seen.

But there was no cessation of the noise, which approached with increasing velocity and was by this time almost abreast of the startled hearers. And now the dumb creatures began to show signs of unmistakable terror: the cows flung their heads high and with piteous bellowing rushed off into the surrounding woods, while the pigs tore around their enclosure, squealing in a most distracted manner.

Only the human creatures stood their ground, with staring eyes which saw nothing, and blanching cheeks that told their fear of this invisible presence. Having arrived at that part of the road opposite the fence, the noise turned, passed through a fence, every rail of which seemed to fall, adding to the horrible confusion, though to the eye all remained secure, traversed the cow yard, struck against the fence which constituted the pigpen, passing in so doing within a few feet of Mr. G, who staggered back and fell to the ground, and then as if its mission were accomplished, it turned off abruptly, ran through another fence, and striking into a unused wood-road, gradually died away.

Meantime, attracted by the noise, Mrs. G came out of the house, calling, "What is the matter? Whose team is running away?" When someone answered they had seen nothing, she grew pale, and exclaimed, "Which one of us does it mean?"

She was known to believe that her family always received some warning of approaching death, though neither her husband nor daughter shared in the superstition. As soon as she learned that the manifestation seemed directed especially against Mr. G, she at once made up her mind that it was he who would be taken. Nor did her fears mislead her, as in ten days from that time the farmer, who was assisting in digging a well on his place, was overwhelmed by the earth caving in and died from the injuries he received.

The Uncanny Attendant

It was in the afternoon of a pleasant day in July that a farmer in Benton County, Iowa, was harvesting his oats, assisted by his two eldest daughters - twins, aged sixteen - and a hired man. The farmer himself had gone to the house on an errand, the young girls and the man remaining at their work. The road lay perhaps a hundred yards from the field where the harvesters were crossing; a short distance from the farm was a small hill.

Presently there appeared on the brow of the hill a pedestrian, the sight of whom, in this sparsely settled country, was enough to make these onlookers view his approach with interest, which presently received a strong stimulus from a singularity in the appearance of the stranger. This was a figure directly behind him, but taller. As it drew near, it presented to the astonished eyes of the harvesters the form of a dark skeleton-like creature, which, following closely in the wake of the stranger, kept step with him and imitated his every movement.

Once, when the apparently unconscious man raised his hand to wipe the perspiration from his forehead, the creature behind, as if the same will governed both, repeated the motion, while at intervals it would crane its long neck forward and peer into the face of the man, as if assuring itself of the identity of its victim or chuckling at having him secure. And so this strangely assorted couple moved along the quiet country road, while the spectators stared aghast, recognizing the fact they were having a glimpse of something mysterious and terrible, but unable to understand what it meant, or why there should have opened to them this one page alone in a perhaps bloody history, for none of the three ever heard or saw more of this pedestrian and his uncanny attendant, who passed quietly from sight as they had come.

At the house, which was still farther from the road, the inmates had remarked on the stranger and had noticed that there was something behind him, but were too far to distinguish anything more and had concluded that it was probably some machinery on his back, but the young girls, one of whom told me the story, and the man knew that it was something resembling a human form, or, rather, an attenuated caricature of one.

The Lost Bracelet

This third circumstance from Ohio, which I will now relate, is rather of the nature of a psychological puzzle and may, of course, be susceptible to explanation by those who have made a study of that strange, unconscious influence which one mind has over another.

My authority for what follows was a niece of the lady who is the principal actor. The lady in question had received as a legacy from a dying relative a handsome massive bracelet of unique design but had it in her possession only a short time when it disappeared.

After a diligent search and many unavailing efforts to ascertain how and by whom it had been stolen, for to that conclusion she was forced, she at last reluctantly abandoned all hope of ever recovering it, and as the years passed on, forgot it, so far as a woman can ever forget the loss of a piece of jewelry which, besides its intrinsic worth, possessed the value of tender associations.

24

One day, some nine or ten years after her loss, she was taking an afternoon nap and dreamed that a lady whom she had long known appeared to her in evident distress, saying, "I want to tell you something," but on the sleeper asking, "Well, what is it?" only repeated, "I want to tell you something."

This dream occurred three times, making, naturally, no little impression on the lady. On awaking, she rose and, leaving her bedroom, passed into an adjoining sitting room. There her eyes fell on some newspapers lying on a chair which stood by an open window, and, with the instinct of an orderly housekeeper, she went to the chair and began gathering up the papers. Underneath them lay a package which, being opened, was found to contain the long-lost bracelet, and with it a slip of paper bearing these words in an unfamiliar writing: "Be sure thy sin will find thee out." I venture to say that no psychological reasoning that could be offered would alter this lady's instantaneous conviction that the woman of her dream was the thief, who, penitent at last, had restored her ill-gotten treasure.

Good News for Ghosts

Many quirky stories in the archives, sadly, never see the light of day. Here is one that certainly made me laugh.

In May 1882, the Daily Telegraph published the following:

> Ghosts of all kinds ought to feel extremely indebted to the Legislature of the State of Ohio in America. That sapient body has decreed that henceforth anybody who claims to be a spiritualist "medium" must pay a yearly tax of forty pounds for permission to practice his so-called profession.
>
> The news will be received with considerable satisfaction in ghostly circles, for the inconvenience to which respectable spirits have often been put in the way of attending séances and rapping tables amounts to a positive scandal. A phantom that had retired for the night was liable to have his legitimate repose disturbed at any moment by the inconsiderate "summons" of a professional spiritualist in the upper world and could hardly call his soul his own.

Maybe this needs to be legislated for ghost walks and ghost hunts?

Des Moines's Plague of Ghosts

May 1878 saw the Iowa town of Des Moines reach fever pitch in alleged spectral activity; from a music box operated by invisible hands, poltergeist activity, and ghosts of children appearing to their parents. The town was overwhelmed with strangeness.

The Des Moines Register was at the forefront of the investigation into the ghostly activity; one correspondent wrote,

> Ever since the Third Street spook raised such a rumor, ghostly visitors appear to have become numerous. Closely following the sudden demise of the uncertain spirit that disturbed the denizens of the Fourth Ward were heard rumors of ghost powers running sewing machines. Several citizens well known testify that the wheels were turned by some unknown and invisible agency.

Possibly the population of Des Moines had become hysterical about ghosts, looking for any small, unusual activity that couldn't be readily explained and attributing it to paranormal activity. Other reports flooded into the newspapers; unnatural green lights were witnessed appearing on walls and invisible bells were heard in the middle of the night.

The Des Moines Register reported,

> A house on Locus Street is afflicted with a bright light shining in a certain place on the wall of a bedroom. The light is plainly visible at a distance but disappears whenever anyone gets close to it. Another peculiarity is that it shines as brightly during the day as night, although it is necessary to close the shutters and darken the room during the sunlight hours in order to see the spook in all its brilliancy.

On Tenth Street in May 1878, dogs were alleged to be witnessing ghosts! One dog would suddenly fiercely attack the air and chase an invisible foe. Another phenomenon claimed to have occurred is that a piano started to play by itself. The witness's daughter, a musician, was absent at the time, but as the witness hurried into the house, he discovered the piano closed and locked.

A lady residing in East Des Moines, because she was very much interested in the Third Street ghost, made several visits to the locality where it was reported to be haunting. One evening, accompanied by several other ladies, she was at the house, returning home about ten o'clock. Two of the ladies went into the parlor with her and sat down to talk over the ghost. Suddenly a large music-box on the mantel commenced to play, continuing through five tunes, the instrument being geared for ten. When it ceased, the box was examined and found to be entirely "run down." It was replaced on the mantel, and a moment later it commenced to play again.

Spectral phenomena seemed rife, albeit strange. The Register continued detailing the reports, including the match-lighting spook that saved its home by lighting a faulty gas light and the lady who shared moments with the ghost of her dead son. She claimed that the ghost would visit the room where her son died and play with his favorite toy.

The ghost phenomenon left Des Moines as quickly as it had come. The following months of the Des Moines Register and national newspapers have no mentions of ghostly activity in the streets and houses of the town. Was it just mass hysteria, or did something really strange happen in this Iowa town?

Shooting a Ghost

In 1867, Mr. Delos was a wealthy and influential man living in a southwestern Ohio town, sadly not named to keep the gentleman's real identity confidential.

On one particular day, Mr. Delos discovered that his only son John had traveled to Cleveland to watch a prize fight between Gallagher and Davis – Ohio's most famous prize fighters at the time. Not only that, but John had helped himself to his father's pocketbook containing two hundred dollars.

This situation threw Mr. Delos into a rage; for the whole day, he complained of a raging headache and began to have the symptoms of a fever. On John's return on Monday afternoon, the old gentleman descended into a fit of rage and grief on hearing that his son had lost one hundred and fifty dollars by betting on the loser, Gallagher.

Finally, the father's rage took him over and he knocked his son to the floor with a blow of his fist, and then immediately fell himself. On being discovered by his family, he was dead. Because blood was flowing from his mouth and nose, the physician concluded that Mr. Delos had died from a burst blood vessel in his brain. Neither the family nor the physician made any effort to resuscitate him, and his remains were prepared for burial.

The following Wednesday, Mr. Delos's body was prepared in a shroud and laid in the coffin; many remarked on the wonderful look of his skin and the color in his face. Delos was a popular and well-loved man. His funeral was well attended, and his remains were temporarily placed in the vaults of the cemetery, as his brick tomb had not been completed.

Within twenty-four hours of the funeral, the village was thrown into excitement because a ghost had been seen in the cemetery and an old lady who had witnessed the ghost had been thrown into a senseless state. As with many ghost sightings of the Victorian age, the villagers believed the ghost was a hoax and set about to find the scoundrel who had played the trick.

Armed with shotguns, the villagers descended on the graveyard, and they did not have long to wait, for there flitting among the tombs was the ghost. With trembling hands and chest-busting beating hearts, they raised their guns and fired at the ghost, and then the white object fell between two graves.

Cautiously, they approached the object lying between the graves and illuminated the "ghost" with the lantern – it was the body of Mr. Delos!

The party lifted Mr. Delos's bloody body and took it home, while some of the party investigated the vaults. There they found Delos's coffin broken open and lying on the floor next to the overturned coffin of a deceased lady, which had been placed on top of it. The vault door had been forced open by the still-alive Delos and he had wandered into the cemetery wearing the shroud, causing the misidentification that he was a ghost.

Delos recovered from his ordeal of being nearly buried alive and shot at! He told his family that on early Thursday evening he awoke and thought he had been buried alive. Determined to escape his coffin, he burst through the wood and wandered in the cemetery, delusional; he didn't understand his situation.

There is no doubt that Mr. Delos had a very unusual experience; not only did he survive possibly being buried alive, but how he didn't receive serious injuries after the shooting is incredible.

Maybe Mr. Delos was lucky after all.

A Live Spook

South Bend, Indiana, once was the home to a very well-behaved spook that intrigued the whole state.

On February 4, 1846, the Monoquet Kosciusko Republican discussed the ghost and its strange activities:

> The rumor that Mr. Coquillard's large mill adjacent to town was haunted has attracted crowds of visitors around it for some time past. The "entertainments" generally consist of sudden flashes of lights through the mill, accompanied with loud noises, intended together to give a faint idea of ghost thunder and lightning.
>
> Public opinion is rather divided as to whether the operator is a live ghost or a live wag, but one evening recently we took a vote of the multitude who were assembled to witness the exciting scene, and a large majority decided it to be a ghost, and no mistake - but a very decent, well-behaved spook, as he neither groans, talks, nor exhibits himself to the awe-struck bystanders.
>
> Those desiring to witness the operations will please visit his headquarters soon, as he will probably before long go into winter quarters. The performances will generally commence between 8 and 9 p.m. every fair evening - and the curtain will drop at exactly 11, unless the largeness of the company will justify its continuance till midnight.

Unlike the brash and loud hoaxing of the time – could this have been some form of real paranormal activity?

And So, It Begins

Mediums, psychics, and clairvoyants are all around us now, but there was once a time when "seers" were a rarity. There have always been old wise women and people who had "strange episodes," but it was in the 1850s that the Fox sisters inspired the spiritualist movement through their public séances, and more and more people came to believe in spiritualism.

However, I want to concentrate on two years earlier, when the alleged phenomenon witnessed at the family home alerted the sisters to their powers. The story would appear in several newspapers across the county:

> The ghostal arrangements which have for some time astonished the good people of Hydesville, Wayne County, and surrounding neighborhood, continue to be the wonder of the day. It seems that the mysterious rapping had been heard for a considerable length of time, to the great terror of the occupants of the house. On the night of the 30th of March, the knocking was much louder than usual, and the family were suddenly awakened by the terrifying shriek of a young lady in the dwelling, who declared that the cold hands of the ghost had been drawn over her face.

The neighbors were called in - a consultation was had, while fear and alarm were visible on every countenance. The lights were extinguished, and in breathless anxiety all awaited the mysterious sounds, the young lady who had received the especial attention of his ghostship still remaining on the bed.

> Soon the rap, rap, rap was heard, and the hairs of their heads resembled so many porcupine quills in stiffness! Finally, the ghost was told that if he really was a spirit, "to rap three times." The mysterious visitor complied, the raps freezing the blood in the veins of the listeners. Other questions were asked and answered in the same way, the spirit informing his audience that it was murdered, and that the body was

32

underneath the ground. It is said, also, that it communicated the important fact, that "Universalism" was false, and that "Methodism was the only true faith." If nothing more is accomplished, the settling of these knotty questions will repay all the trouble that the neighborhood has been put to.

The excitement now waxed high, and crowds visited the haunted house. The first day of April witnessed a continued going and coming, near the scene of the mystery, and in order to solve the matter, resort was had to a fortune teller near at hand. A well-worn pack of cards were produced, and the first "cut" was the Jack of Hearts, showing that a murder had been committed! The next brought out the "deuce," indicating the victim was low, that is, buried in the cellar!

Once more the mystic oracle was consulted, and the nine of spades came forth from the pack, furnishing the most conclusive testimony that the murdered man was nine feet underground.

Again the "deck" was cut, and the ace of diamonds was presented to their protruding eyes, indicative that the murdered man was possessed of a large amount of money! Here was the evidence the most conclusive, and the excitement spread.

Several individuals immediately commenced digging for bones in the spot indicated and after reaching a depth of four or five feet, a clairvoyant in the neighborhood communicated the vexatious intelligence that the bones had been removed and cast into the water of the Ganargwa! Thus, according to the pamphlet from which we gather these particulars, the whole matter remains an impenetrable mystery.

The Return of Dr. Jewel

In the St. Anthony area of Minneapolis there was great excitement that the Winslow House Hotel was haunted. Built in 1857, the Winslow House Hotel was considered one of the finest hotels in the nation. It was a popular hotel built to serve visitors to St. Anthony Falls; however, with the onset of the Civil War, the hotel lost much of its clientele and closed its doors. In the 1860s, the hotel passed through several owners' hands, but in 1868 it was owned by Dr. Jewel and housed a series of businesses and apartments. By 1886, the building, being in a dilapidated state, was torn down to make way for the Exposition Building and later the Coca-Cola plant construction. Sadly, this haunted hotel is now a parking lot.

For this case, let us return to 1868. Professor F. E. Bain, who resided in the building, reported to local newspapers that a series of strange sights and sounds had been seen and heard.

Professor Bain gave this statement to the Minneapolis Tribune on March 22, 1868, which at the time was a bold declaration, especially considering his standing:

The Winslow House is a very large building lately run and occupied by the late Dr. Jewel who died some eight or ten weeks since. In his lifetime, the house was used as a water-cure establishment, but since his death it has been closed, and with the exception of the room occupied by his widow and her family, and those occupied by myself and family and two other families, the house is tenantless.

The doctor, before his death, frequently said he would revisit the house to see how things were getting along, but no attention was paid to these remarks, which were generally made while suffering from excruciating pain. His wife and family, however, cherished the words in their memory and frequently repeated them to their intimate friends.

He (the doctor) did not, however, show himself until Saturday 14th when Mrs. Jewel had advertised for sale by auction all her furniture, bedding, etc., which is to take place on the 24th. In the center part of the building on the ground floor are cellars, laundry, etc. and in one of these rooms a steam engine, which had been used for heating, pumping water, etc. but all the belting had been removed and the engine out of use for years past. The first thing that attracted the attention of myself and the neighbors was the occasional running of the wheel upon which the belts used to be placed. This seemed strange, but we said little about it, for fear of being laughed at by our neighbors.

On Saturday morning, the 14th, my daughter, an intelligent girl of fourteen years of age, was returning from the post office (which, by the way, is kept in a room on the ground floor, in the southeast corner of the building) and came through the room in which the engine stands, and there saw a tall, slim man dressed in a fine suit of broadcloth, with a white night-cap on his head, and a pair of white stockings on his feet.

She passed him without speaking and came into the house and made the remark to her mother and myself that a strange looking man was walking through the laundry, dressed as above, and that he must be a fool.

This was about 10 o'clock a.m., and I went out with her to see the man whom she described as looking and acting so strangely. When we went out nothing was to be seen, and we went and looked through the largest cellar, a dark and bleak apartment forty feet long, by about twenty wide - when all at once she exclaimed, "Father! There he is coming toward us!" and began to draw me back to the door by the hand and seemed to be very nervous.

I could see nothing, but supposing it was someone who was trying to frighten us, I demanded in an angry voice, "Who is here? What do you want?" I received no reply - yet the strange appearance passed out of the cellar within two feet of us, as it appeared to her. We went into the next house, and myself and Mr. Hubert, my next-door neighbor, got a lamp and made a thorough search of all the premises, but neither saw nor heard anything. That evening we again explored the dark and dreary cellars etc. in company with another man, and at the extremity of the interior cellar, in a dark corner, found a large towel, clean and ironed, as if dropped by someone.

This towel belonged to Mrs. Jewel and had been washed and laid by about a month ago. We then concluded that our visitor was flesh and blood, and that his visits wore not an honest character. Under this belief, both Mr. Hubert and I came to the conclusion that we would bring his ghostship to grief, and for the benefit of all concerned gave due notice accordingly – Mr. Hubert got his revolver in readiness and gave my daughter one also, but that night all was still, nothing seen or heard.

On Sunday morning we were congratulating ourselves that our threats of vengeance dire had had the desired effect but about ten o'clock a.m. our hopes were dispelled by the loud report of a pistol and the piercing cry of "Oh, my God!" I had instructed my daughter that in case she should see him again to shoot him instantly if he would not speak, and that I would stand between her and any harm. She went to the laundry door for the broom, having her pistol in her pocket, and just inside of the door stood the man, looking directly at her in the same garb in which she first saw him. She immediately drew the pistol and presented it at him, but he seemed indifferent to the weapon and at the distance of six feet she fired at him. He at once bent forward, clasping his hands across his breast, exclaiming, "Oh, my God!" and disappeared into the cellar.

I heard the report of the pistol and heard the cry of "Oh, my God!" and under the impression that she had shot herself, I ran to the door, when she exclaimed, "Father, I have shot him; he is in the cellar," and as we were going in, she said, "Oh, Father, I have killed him! What shall I do?" We looked for the man, searched for traces of blood, but to our great surprise and consternation found neither.

On Monday, while placing the clothes on the line in the yard, she saw him again. When she asked him who he was, and what he wanted, he looked at her in a very imploring manner and after having surveyed her attentively asked, "What is your name?" She replied that her name was A. E. Bain. He then in a clear, shrill voice said, "Go to No. 47 on the fourth story, and see what you can see!"

She in company with several others went to the room indicated, but neither saw nor heard anything. This, be it remembered, was at mid-day in open daylight, with a clear Minnesota sky, and the sun shining brightly. She did not even know that there was such a number in the house on the fourth story. When I asked her why she did not at this interview shoot him, she said that he looked so pitiful that she could not find it in heart to do so. On Thursday, the 10th, saw him again, but as he was rapidly gliding through the cellar door she missed him, lodging a bullet in the wall. Half an hour later she saw him again, whom he beckoned her to him, and told her to tell Mrs Jewel "to sit on the west side of the table when she held the next séance," and then disappeared.

Mrs. Jewel, who is a practicing physician and a highly educated lady, myself, and my daughter went down but could see or hear nothing. Now, my daughter never saw Dr. Jewel during his life, and to rest the matter, Dr. Thomas W. Deering took the photographs of seventeen different persons, all men, among which was one of the late Dr. Jewel, and placed them before her, and asked her, "Are any of these like the man whom you saw?" After looking them over carefully, she took Jewel's likeness, taken shortly before his death, and said, "Oh, there is the man, I know his face, eyes, and beard."

Dr. Jewel was interred in his wedding suit, and although she did not see him at any time in his life or know how he was dressed when placed in the coffin, her description was true to the very buttons on his coat.

Several men, on Friday night last, paid a visit to the laundry, but beat a hasty retreat having to encounter attacks of a dreadful dog with fiery eyes and savage mane, and they declared it was really a dog and thought that he belonged to the house, but there is no dog about the premises.

The Tribune concluded the letter with the following statement:

> Professor McBain and Mr. Hubert relate many circumstances quite unaccountable and tell us that their statements can be substantiated by others who have been eyewitnesses. Neither Professor McBain nor his daughter to whom the apparition appeared are believers in modern spiritualism. On the contrary, their opinions are very strongly against, and they are not liable, therefore, to be easily misled or deceived.

> The widow of Dr. Jewel is a firm believer in spiritualism as are a number of relatives and friends, and at the séances, frequently held, they have received what purported to be communications from the deceased doctor, stating that he

had in reality appeared to Miss McBain, and was often in and about the building.

And so, I thought the story finished. However, by a stroke of luck I received very recently another clipping stating that the Winslow House Hotel hauntings continued after this initial article.

Professor McBain wrote,

> Since the first announcement of ghostly appearances at the Winslow House, in St. Anthony, hundreds of people have visited the building, and occupants of the house state that the strange sights and sounds have often been repeated. As the manifestations were very similar to those spoken of in our first account, we have not referred to them, but the following statement in reference to occurrences on last Sunday morning, verified by three witnesses, will be read with interest.

I have abbreviated the following statement, mainly due to the long-winded descriptions, but it retains the statement's message:

> On Sunday morning last, at about half-past eight o'clock, I met a gentleman from Stearns County, by the name of (Samuel) Secord, who came down to see if he could not solve the mystery connected with the "Winslow House Ghost." He told me his business and requested me to show him through the haunted portions of the house.

> He is a strong believer in spiritualism and displayed a good deal of enthusiasm in its advocacy and felt confident that the apparitions which had been previously were from the spirit world. On our way to the engine room, we met Mr. Hubert, who accompanied us. We went thro' all the cellar rooms and holes in the lower part of the building, and all was as silent as the tomb; not a sound was heard, nor anything seen until we went into the room on the northwest corner of the building, in which stands a large, heavy table. When we entered this

room, the door closed behind us, and owing to the fact that the inside knob was off the lock, I, in a joking manner, remarked that we had closed ourselves in, and would have a poor chance to beat a hasty retreat. I scarcely made the remark when a tall, ghastly-looking man entered the room.

"In the name of God, doctor, what do you want?" exclaimed Mr. Hubert.

I had never seen Dr. Jewel in my life before, and while he was meditating on his answer to Mr. Hubert's question, I noticed his appearance was not in the point of materially like anything earthly. It seemed to lack weight and substance and more resembled the gravity and movement of a very dense and heavy shadow. His movements were noiseless and graceful, and he seemed to slide rather than walk and looked like a man on skates with both feet together under very slow motion. After a pause of a few seconds he said, "I have a message to communicate and have hitherto failed to get anyone to whom I can unbosom my troubles, because they seem to fear me and in conclusion leave me or forget to ask me the question which you have done. My troubles are concerning my wife and daughter who are shortly going to California and unless they take this warning, they will be both lost. The steamer that will be waiting for them on the Pacific, after being three days out, will be destroyed by fire, and many lives lost. They must not go on that vessel, but on another of smaller dimensions which will safely reach its destination.

The communication between the ghost of Mr. Jewel and Mr. Hubert and McBain continues and McBain comments,

The most singular part of this affair is that although Mr. Secord was standing between Mr. Hubert and myself, he saw nothing, though he distinctly heard all that was said. He attempted to elicit some information from him concerning dead relations, but he seemed not to heed Mr. Secord's interrogations at all. His voice was subdued and clear, and his words were articulated with a marked precision that indicated

41

harbored effort, and each sentence was followed by a long pause, as if he was pondering over the next sentence before uttering it.

He then vanished but did not go out of the door…We are satisfied that there was no optical delusion, no working of the imagination, but that we all both saw and heard what is herein stated.

For days I have borne the laughter and jeers of many from whom better things might have been expected, but all the harm I wish them is, that they had been present at that interview.

After the second statement, I found myself questioning the authenticity of the statements from McBain and Hubert. Was it "real" communication with a frustrated spirit or an elaborate hoax by McBain and Hubert? The fact that Secord did not witness the ghost and only heard the communication possibly highlights that it could have been a hoax.

The question is why Professor McBain, a self-proclaimed skeptic, would actually perpetrate a hoax, especially with his standing in the community. Was he a convert to spiritualism, or merely someone looking for fame and money?

Sadly, we will never know; unlike many ghost scares of the time, the Winslow House hauntings never grabbed the media's attention and disappeared into the background.

Unlike the Fox and Bangs sisters (see stories "And So it begins" and "A Séance too far"), the story never progressed from being a "haunted house" story into demonstrations of spiritualism or mediumship. Maybe this gives authenticity to the hauntings and maybe the McBains really did experience the ghost of Dr. Jewel in 1868.

Forbes Manor

Forbes Manor near Albany is not only of historical importance, but also is the scene of a very unusual tale and haunting.

Originally built by the Van Rensselaer family in 1842 as a palatial country mansion set in hundreds of acres of land, the Van Rensselaer sadly did not live there very long. Within five years, the "Anti-Rent War" forced then owner William Paterson van Rensselaer to sell his lands and mansion since they were no longer bringing in rent. The price was greatly reduced, and Paul S. Forbes, a wealthy New York City merchant, purchased the estate and its nine hundred acres.

Now known as Forbes Manor, this beautiful, grand mansion for reasons unknown was not inhabited by the Forbes for very long.

In 1860, Forbes Manor was the scene of many a social gathering. On one particular night during this year when the manor house was full of people for a gathering like no other, with drinks flowing and people dancing, something happened, something unexplained. The night after the gala all the servants, except four faithful who had been with the family for years, were discharged, and shortly after breakfast all the members of the family left the manor house in their carriages. No goodbyes were said. Behind them they left their beautiful home as it had been the day before. On the mantels and dressers were pictures of friends and family, and in the drawers and wardrobes were their clothes, on the desks their letters and papers. The doors were locked, the curtains drawn, and the house closed.

The house was abandoned for decades; the estate was used for picnics, baseball matches, and sometimes gypsy encampments! The mansion slowly fell into disrepair until it was purchased by the Order of Franciscans for St. Anthony-on-the-Hudson Seminary, which still owns it today.

A story ran in many newspapers in 1890 claiming that the manor's ghost was a man in black believed to walk the house every night, mumbling as he passes up and down the broad stairway. Scores of people claimed to have heard him and a few said they had seen him.

One of witness described him as follows:

His hair was long and curly and parted on the side, his eyes were bright, his features clearly cut and his face pale. He was smooth shaven and wore a high standing collar and a black bow and stock. He was in evening dress and wore no jewelry except a gold fob. For a moment he ceased mumbling and then began moaning and walked away. He passed the door, walking toward the stairway.

The ghost then climbed the stairs only to fall halfway to the top, his head striking one of the marble steps before he vanished.

In 1900, further insights into the haunts of the Forbes Manor were published by the New Castle News, when it discussed a ball to take place at the deserted mansion house,

Albany's select set will give a colonial dance on the evening of December 19 in a deserted and haunted house. Tradition says the place is haunted. All sorts of mysterious noises have been heard, and some persons hint at lights in the windows which have revealed forms. There is a sealed chamber which is a potent argument in favor of many rumors.

Also, there is a dark stain on the landing of the grand staircase, and tradition says it is blood; that toward the close of the eighteenth century on December 19, the manor was the scene of a brilliant ball which terminated with a duel on the staircase.

The night of December 19 therefore is the time when superstitious persons are afraid to go near the old mansion.

It seems that that the private purchase of Forbes Manor not only rescued a historic house for future generations but took away the chance to investigate this old and intriguing haunting.

Ghosts In The Capitol

In 1891, it was claimed that the Capitol building had fifteen ghosts wandering its corridors. The most infamous of the Capitol's ghosts is the Demon Cat; it was claimed that the cat "possesses much more remarkable features than any of the others, insomuch as it has the appearance of an ordinary pussy when first seen, and presently swells up to the size of an elephant before the eyes of the terrified observer."

A sighting of the demon cat was first recorded in 1802 when one of the watchmen on duty in the building shot at it, and then it disappeared. Since its first sighting, the demon cat has become a legend. According to tradition, the cat is seen before presidential elections and tragedies in Washington DC, allegedly being spotted before the assassinations of John F. Kennedy and Abraham Lincoln.

The U.S. Capitol Historical Society has claimed to have "laid to rest the demon cat" with the explanation that the original sighting was witnessed by a security guard who was licked by a cat while he was lying down. Being drunk, the man thought that he was still standing at the time and was frightened by an apparently giant cat! Steve Livengood of the society claimed, "eventually the other guards found out that they could get a day off if they saw the demon cat" and hence it's journey into legend.

But what about some of the other fourteen ghosts said to wander the building?

One of the most curious and alarming phenomena observed by the night watchmen is a ghostly footstep that follows anybody who crosses Statuary Hall at night. It was in this hall, then the chamber of the House of Representatives, that John Quincy Adams died – at a spot indicated now by a brass tablet set in a stone slab, where stood his desk.

Whether or not it is Adams's ghost that pursues the watchmen is open to debate, but with ghost sightings continuing in Statuary Hall to modern day, it certainly asks the question, why?

Working for most of his adult life in the Library of Congress, Mr. Twine would spend the day stamping books with a mixture of alcohol and lampblack in an office resembling a large iron cage. Long after the library moved and Twine's death, he continued revisiting his office. Guards would hear his rubber meeting the book, and they knew Twine was back on his old stamping ground.

Another ghost resides beneath the hall of the House of Representatives and strolls by night. He is described as "an erect figure, a great mustache, and his hand clasped behind him. Who he is nobody has even surmised; he might be, judging from his aspect, a foreigner in the diplomatic service?" Over the years many watchmen have approached this spectral intruder, but it disappears from sight.

During the 1890s, it was believed that at 12:30 every night, the door of the room occupied by the committee on military affairs would open and the figure of General John A. Logan would step forth. Logan is instantly recognizable by his long black hair, military attire, and the hat he was accustomed to wear in life. He was once chairman of the committee and, if reports were to be believed, was still supervising matters ten years after his death. Logan's ghost was reported to walk down the marble-floored corridor, but no one has followed him, so no one knows where he goes; he just never walks back!

One spectral visitor was the ghost of former Vice President Henry Wilson, who died in the Senate wing in 1875. Contemporary reports said that his ghost almost frightened to death a watchman guarding the coffin of a Tennessee senator lying in state in the Senate chamber.

Another phenomenon that has appeared to the cleaners and morning shift workers is that of a cleaner who died many years ago. In winter when the early hours are dark, cleaners would see the specter of the cleaner scrubbing away at the floors for many hours. Not only could witnesses see the ghost, but as he sunk his brush into his pail and splashed the suds onto the floor, the sound was clearly audible.

This may be just a legend, but the "Walled-Up Workman" was thought to be a laborer sealed behind masonry during construction of the Capitol. Passersby could hear the unfortunate fellow's ghost scraping with a trowel to draw attention, but it never got so bad that any walls were torn down to free him!

There are many ghosts in the Capitol building and its surroundings; with such an incredible history and saturation of human emotions, is it any wonder that the politicians and workers who once worked in the building return in the afterlife?

Jonelle Lambkin Rings the Bell

There are many tales where the spirit of a person cannot rest so it returns to the earthly plains to exact revenge or set things right. This may be the case in our following story.

In 1894, a ghost began to cause havoc within a small community in Lincoln, Arkansas. The locals believed the ghost to be of a woman named Jonelle Lambkin, who was thrown out of church for some unknown misdemeanor. She had died a few months previously but with her dying breath she exclaimed that she was a wrongfully accused woman and the community would receive proof of this!

Soon after her death, every night, the specter of a woman in white manifested in the belfry of the church and rang the bell three times before disappearing. The mystery of this ghost caused great upset and puzzlement among the community of Lincoln, for the only approach to the belfry was a stairway to which entrance is gained by a single door. Not only that, but the door was also guarded every night since the commencement of the mysterious tolling.

A crowd would appear to witness the ghost, and more than a hundred people would watch the staircase door and still she appeared. The staircase and belfry were searched every time she rang the bell – and still found empty.

> Besides, the belfry is only large enough to hold the bell itself, and when that is in motion there is no footing for a person. The rope that is ordinarily employed in ringing the bell hangs all the time in plain view of the crowd and is perfectly motionless. The woman is also distinctly visible, but whether white or black it is impossible to tell. Even if the figure itself was a figment of the imagination, the ringing of the bell is not, as that is to be unmistakably heard for a quarter of a mile, wrote the Greeley Tribune.

Did Jonelle continue her nightly tolls, or had she provided enough evidence of her innocence to the community of Lincoln, Arkansas?

Sadly, we will never know; Jonelle's specter, like many in this book, disappeared and was never heard from again.

Mrs. Warfield's Haunted House

In Cincinnati on 5th Street once stood a brick house of three stories containing a storeroom and eight or ten large rooms. The widow Mrs. Warfield owned the property, which was constantly let to one tenant after another, often tenants changing within days of moving in.

On September 22, 1852, the Times & Press of Fort Wayne reported a series of strange occurrences at the building when Mr. Edwards and his family took residence at the house.

Edwards had only been in the house a few days when at about 10 o'clock, a noise similar to the discharge of a pistol was heard in an upper front room; however, on examination no cause for the report could be found. A few hours later, after the family and boarders had retired to bed, the inhabitants heard a succession of gun shots, as well as loud screams from the room of several young women boarders who were sleeping.

The whole house was awakened, and several people rushed to the origin of the sound. As they rushed into the female boarders' room, the young women were discovered to be in a state of absolute terror. They claimed the pistol shots were made at their bedside and repeated that, as if from a revolver, they also witnessed flashes of red light following each report. One girl was pale and senseless from the fright and told reporters that she had witnessed a tall, dark figure stooped over her pillow.

On the following day at noon, another sharp shot was heard in the kitchen and for several hours during the day a noise was heard in the dining room resembling the pawing of a horse or banging of a hammer. Mr. Edwards decided to seek another house for his family, and his boarders refused to sleep another night in the house.

Unusually, it was Mrs. Warfield who also hit the headlines with her reaction to Mr. Edwards's claims.

The Times & Press reported the following:

> The owner of the property threatens to sue the tenant for damages in giving the house the character of being "haunted" by circulating tales, and leaving the place, while Mr. Edwards thinks that damages should be given him, insomuch as he was not informed of the reports previous to his renting it, which he understands currently believed in the neighborhood regarding its "ghosts." Not only has the matter taken this phase, but the present lessee, upon the same grounds, demands the annulling of his contract, and so all that have been concerned in the building are asking reparation for their losses.

The neighbors of the house believed it to be haunted by the spirit of a murdered carpenter looking for revenge, while others believed it was a rich benefactor whose will had been destroyed with designs to defraud an orphan girl. The benefactor's ghost is believed to create the noises to bring the orphan's plight to people's attention.

Whether Mrs. Warfield's claim was upheld in a court we do not know but based on the few references to the hauntings of the 5th Street house, there seems to be enough evidence that it was known for being haunted – by a noisy, gun-firing poltergeist.

Mumler's Spirit Photography

In 1863, Boston inhabitant William H. Mumler claimed to be on the verge of discovering a "chemical test for ghosts" and to have discovered a chemical means of identifying them. Mumler told the international media that he had discovered "spirit photography" and that ghosts under certainly magnetic conditions affect the nitrate of silver, even when they are invisible to the human eye.

Mumler was interviewed by the British magazine The Spectator in March 1863:

> Mumler is a powerful 'medium,' being a rich reservoir of Od force. Last year he was taking a photograph of himself when, to his great astonishment, on 'developing' the picture, he perceived in the chair on which his hand had been leaning another figure which was not visibly with him when he was operating. He recognized her as a deceased relative of his own, who died at about twelve or fourteen years of age, which age she still appears to retain.

The article describes how Mumler, since his discovery, had become besieged "not merely by sitters, but, unfortunately also by 'investigators.'"

Mumler wrote, "Ever since I have commenced taking these pictures, I have been constantly dodged forward and backward from my camera to my closet by investigators, till I have become sick of the name."

Indeed, the "investigators" were split in their conclusions about Mumler's photography. Mr William Guay, a well-known "photographic artist" of the time, believed that the photographs were authentic; however he was a well-known spiritualist as well (and later became Mumler's business partner). The American Photographic Society, meeting in New York, resolved that the "spiritual likenesses are a fraud and a gross deception" and the Evening Post delivered a similar opinion.

Over the next six years, Mumler established studios in Boston and then New York; he also traveled the U.S. taking "spirit photographs" mainly for those who had lost family members in the Civil War. Some even said that his popularity was purely down to taking advantage of those grieving (similar words were uttered in England after World War I when spiritualism became popular in the 1920s). During these six years, Mumler gained notoriety, taking photographs of the public, mediums, and even minor celebrities of the day.

Soon Mumler's popularity caught up with him; maybe he became lax in his methods but there were rumors that he was a fraud.

In 1869, a legal case was brought against William H. Mumler by the "People of America"; it was without precedent and generated international interest. The charge against Mumler was that what he termed "spiritual photographs" served to swindle many credulous persons and lead them to believe it was possible to photograph "immaterial forms of their departed friends."

Mumler had come to the attention of the mayor of New York when the mayor received a complaint from a visitor to the city who had been photographed in Mumler's studios. In July 1869, the Illustrated Photographer claimed,

> He had gone to a person named Mumler, who practiced in New York as a 'Spiritual photographer' and had paid him ten dollars for a portrait of his deceased grandmother. He was so much gratified with this work of art that he returned to Mumler's shop to order a portrait of another deceased relation, but he encountered at the door a man who was affectionately contemplating the features of his grandmother, which had just been produced by the same process and at the same price. The man found to his astonishment and disgust that not only the process and the price, but the features in the two portraits were the same.

Based on this information and the rumors surrounding Mumler, the mayor asked Marshal Joseph H. Tooker to investigate the claims against Mumler.

Tooker assumed a false name and had his photograph taken by Mumler. After taking the picture, Mumler showed Tooker the negative and there could be seen a dim, indistinct outline of a ghostly face staring out of one corner. Mumler told Tooker that he was looking at the spirit of his father-in-law; however, Tooker failed to recognize the old gentleman in the photograph. Tooker emphatically denied that the picture represented his father-in-law, any of his relations, or any person that he had ever seen!

The most damning fact of all is that Marshal Tooker's father-in-law was alive at the time. Tooker brought the case to the courts and made international headlines.

During the case the counsel for the defense brought forward several witnesses who testified to the genuineness of the photographs. They included fellow photographers and advocates of the spiritualist movement. Judge Edmonds, one of the defense's witnesses even admitted that "the spirit form in one of them (photographs) he could recognize, but not the one in the other."

This appeared in the Morning Standard:

> The device of the charlatan consisted in his executing photographs of living sitters, who paid an extra price for the portrait of some lost relative or friend which should appear plainly recognizable, though in ghostly presence, on the same picture. Many specimens were produced in court. Sorrowing widows, in decorous mourning garb, were taken with the simulacra of their lamented husbands rising over them. Mothers, with the apparitions of departed children in their laps.

The Illustrated Photographer also waded into the argument:

> He had been believed in, in the first place, by a large number of people. He had long obtained, again, a good price for his

photographs; for who could expect spirits to be called 'from the vasty deep' for less than ten dollars per head?

Witness after witness was brought into the courtroom but none made as big an impact as one, the much-celebrated P. T. Barnum, showman and museum owner. In his testimony, Barnum claimed that a few years previously he had been writing a book on humbugs (hoaxes) which became Humbugs of the World. During his composing, he wrote to Mumler to purchase specimens of his "spirit photographs" for the Museum of Humbugs. Accordingly, for two dollars each, Mumler provided a series of "spirit photographs" that featured Napoleon Bonaparte and Henry Clay. Barnum took pains to highlight that the "spirits" of the historical figures were exactly like the well-known photographs that Mumler produced for the public.

The court case was well reported, and various photographic societies and indeed respected photographers reported on it in their magazines and newspapers. Abraham Bogardus, a photographer for twenty-three years, came forward as a witness to offer expert advice. He had known of Mumler and devised several processes by which "spirit photographs" could be created and taken by the dozens.

Bogardus said in court,

> They are made by taking a plate and coating it the usual way, having an impression taken by any camera out of reach or sight of the sitter, and then putting the plate back into the coating bath, it might be left there long as you like, and when a sitter comes it can be used, and the first impression will appear with the figure of the sitter.

Essentially, he described a double exposure. Bogardus also examined several of Mumler's photographs that had been submitted as evidence; discussing one such photograph, Bogardus said,

> It is, so to speak, emphatically, a transparent lie on its face, the shadow on the sitter being on one side, the shadow of the spirit on the other; it shows that two pictures have been taken at different times.

No matter his skepticism, he admitted that no likeness of a person could be produced after death without a copy from life. Either Mumler was photographing "spirit", or he was somehow obtaining photographs of his client's dead relations.

To prove that Bogardus was correct in his assumptions, P. T. Barnum visited his studio and returned to court with a photograph showing him seated with the "spirit" of Abraham Lincoln. Furthermore, Bogarus challenged Barnum and others to identify by which trick he had produced the "spirit"; although they witnessed the entire process from the plate-cleaning to the developing, they failed to discover his plan.

With a huge amount of evidence and numerous witness statements that pointed to Mumler creating an elaborate plan to swindle the public, on May 4, Judge Dowling brought the case to an abrupt end.

In a statement he said,

> After a careful and thorough analysis of this interesting and, I may say, extraordinary case, I have come to the conclusion that the prisoner should be discharged. I will state that, however, I am morally convinced that there may be fraud and deception practiced by the prisoner, yet I sitting as a magistrate to determine from the evidence given by the witnesses according to law, am compelled to decide that I would not be justified in sending this complaint to the Grand Jury, as in my opinion, the prosecution has failed to make out the case. I therefore dismiss the complaint and order the discharge of the prisoner.

This abrupt conclusion to the Mumler case brought derision from the media and commentators of the day. Even after expert witness statements, the experiences of Marshal Tooker should have been evidence enough that Mumler was defrauding the public.

The New Philadelphia Ohio Democrat wrote about the case,

It has been shown by accomplished experts that these so-called spirit photographs can readily be taken by ordinary mechanical and scientific means; and this fact alone ought to prevent people from investigating in similar or poorer pictures which profess to be 'spiritual.'

The Democrat's summing up of the case was surprisingly prophetic. Within seven days of the court hearing, Mumler's lease on his New York studio expired. He returned to Boston and began taking spirit photographs again. Between 1869 and 1875, Mumler took some of his most famous photographs, including one of Mary Todd, Abraham Lincoln's widow.

According to notes of William Stainton Moses, a spiritualist, in 1872 Mary Todd assumed the name "Mrs. Lindall" and visited Mumler's studio. Moses claimed that Mumler only discovered that she was Lincoln's widow after the photograph was developed. Although the image is another double exposure, it shows Abraham Lincoln with his hands on Mary's shoulders looking pensive; it has widely appeared in newspapers, magazines, and books.

In 1875, Mumler published "The personal experiences of William H. Mumler in spirit-photography," a booklet in which he gloated about the legal case against him and the prosecution's witnesses.

However, the case continued to take its toll on his business, reputation, and finances. Mumler never recovered from the staggering cost of $3,000 for his defense lawyer, and by the time he died in 1884 he was penniless. Strangely, he destroyed all his negatives shortly before his death, sealing the enigma that is William H. Mumler's "spirit photography."

Scared to Death by a Ghost

A wealthy Kentucky woman succumbed to a strange case of fright claimed the Fort Wayne Weekly Breeze in September of 1889,

> One of the richest women in the state of Kentucky died at her home in Bellevue. Her funeral was one of the largest seen for many years due to her position and the circumstances of her death. Mrs. Angelo Rusconi was frightened to death by a ghost.
>
> For some time, an "uncanny" visitor had appeared nightly in a room over "Boro's Grocery" on Front Street and crowds gathered nightly to see it. On a Saturday night, Mrs. Rusconi went to see the "ghost." She was very fleshy and was afflicted with a tumor. When suddenly the ghost appeared, she fell dead. A thorough investigation found that the "ghost" was a reflection of an electric light at the river landing.

Further research into her death shows that the Mrs. Ruconi was very much interested in ghosts and asked her friend to drive her to the haunting.

> For a while the crowd stood silently awaiting the spector's appearance. Suddenly it appeared, a white, ghostly thing. With a shriek, Mrs. Rusconi fell unconscious to the floor of her carriage. Her friend drove home as rapidly as possible, but life was extinct.

The stress of her health condition no doubt added to the terror of seeing the 'ghost' and sadly Mrs. Rusconi never saw the success of her grandchild who became a world renown tenor.

The Bones of Timothy Felt

Our oldest ghost story takes place on Mount Tom in the north part of West Springfield MA in 1828. During the building of the New Haven and Northampton Canal many tons of limestone was needed for the creation of cement. Mount Tom was one of the largest quarries with hundreds of men employed all day round to produce the cement. At night some of the men would tend the lime kilns, taking turns in shifts. During one of these shift changes 'appalling and unearthly' sounds and accompanied by the sighting of a ghost.

Over a few nights, the alarm became so great among the workmen, and the ghostly appearances increasing night by night that soon no workmen dare not maintain his post at the kiln. Of course, this concerned the bosses of the quarry, and a watchman was brought in from especially from New York to protect the workforce and investigate the ghost.

The Annapolis Maryland Republican wrote about the reaction of the New York watchman,

> "On hearing their dreadful tale, (he) laughed their fear to scorn, and boldly offered to take a tour upon the haunted spot, promising if anything appeared whether it were a 'spirit of health or goblin damned,' he would speak to it."

The watchman had been at the kilns for a few nights when the ghost wandered into the quarry. What he reported to his colleagues scared them further.

Like others he heard the strange and unusual sounds, then out of the darkness came the specter of headless man. As he promised, the watchman held his nerve and asked the ghost what he wanted?

Even though the ghost was headless it told the man he was the ghost of Timothy Felt, and that he was murdered three years ago. The ghost explained his mortal remains were concealed in a particular fissure of a particular rock in the quarry. The ghost described it with great minuteness and detail that he told the watchman to search for the spot, and bones would be found which would give confirmation of his death and the murderers would confess their deed.

Superstition and fear of the supernatural was rife amongst the workmen of the quarry, while many did not believe the night watchman, they all agreed that a search for the bones must take place.

In daylight (of course), they set out and found the precise rock, containing the precise fissure but discovered no bones. Strangely investigations by journalists into the ghost uncovered another fact, Timothy Felt was the name of a man who did actually disappear in an unaccountable manner three years since. Timothy did exist (one time), and the watchman could not have known about him.

Did the miners and the watchman find the bones? Was Timothy's ghost laid to rest? Sadly, no further records exist, except for Clifton Johnson's "What They Say in New England; A Book of Signs, Sayings and Superstitions" (1896). The author, I believe, creates the back story to Timothy's life, that offensively he was a stupid Irish boy murdered by his father, when actually Timothy told the watchman 'His murderers would confess their deed.'

Clifton wrote about the incident, "This story ran through all the country round, and created great excitement. Every day, for some time afterwards, loads of people, not only from nearby but from towns quite distant, wended their way thither, inquiring the way to the "ghost place;" and when night came on people would make a long detour rather than pass the spot, and run the risk of meeting Tim's skeleton should [he] be bought to light, but no bones were found; and after the overseer had gotten out what stone he wanted, the work lagged and was discontinued.

A Louisville Ghost Hunt

On October 5, 1869, the Louisville Courier Journal published details of a mysterious haunted house. Although the newspaper was very skeptical in its beliefs, there seems to be a real mystery behind the haunting:

> The haunted house we hear about as being located within the corporate limits of Louisville may yet be explained away and converted into a rentable property.
>
> This house, at which we arrive by a route so circuitous, is downtown. We do not choose to give it a particular location, and care nothing for the sneers of the incredulous, who would insinuate that because the number and street are not mentioned the house exists only in the brain of some overworked reporter.
>
> The house can certainly be seen, and if the ghost is as certain as the house, there can be no doubt of the truth of the stories told by housewives, and others in the neighborhood of the property.
>
> It is alleged that there is certainly something wrong with the house, for perhaps no other building in the city, of its age has had as many different tenants. The house is a two-story structure, and every now and then the blinds will be thrown open, curtains will appear in the windows, and the smoke of the kitchen fire rolls out of a portly chimney. This is a sign that a tenant has been found. After a lapse of a day or two, the curtains come down, the blinds come together with a bang, the air above the chimney is clear, and a big wagon, full of furniture, moves solemnly away from the front. Then the tenant is gone. It may be that he has not advanced rent, or it may be half a dozen other things, but he comes and goes, and others come and go, and the haunted house remains without a tenant.

One of the large rooms in the house is the subject of neighborhood gossip, and strange, weird sights are said to have been seen in this room. Some time ago a committee of twelve stout men, more familiar with the yielding qualities of beefsteak than the conventionalities of spiritual society, were detailed to visit the house and occupy the haunted room until the ghost should appear.

The night they attended was a stormy one; howling wind and rain bore down on the party and they reached the house in time for the bells to be striking twelve. These would-be ghost hunters sat quietly for a few minutes, when one of them shouted,

"There she comes!"

As he spoke, there was a light rumbling sound like that of carriage wheels, and it was strangely clear and distinct above the noise of the storm. On the instant the lights in the room sank down, and a light mist filled the apartment. Every object in it could be distinctly seen, however, as the lights were not totally extinguished, and the vapor itself did not tend to darken the room. The twelve strained their eyes, and some of them sat open-mouthed. As the vapor appeared, the sound of carriage wheels became louder, and in a moment, to the horror of the committee, a carriage itself, black as a hearse, came rolling into the middle of the room and stopped. No horses were visible, but as soon as the roll of the wheels had ceased a figure resembling that of a lady, clad in white, suddenly appeared and was seen to step into the strange vehicle.

Then the carriage wheeled off and was seen no more.

The Louisville Courier Journal admitted that while the story was "very much enlarged upon, that something very strange had happened in the house. The house is quite valuable, but no tenant has yet to be found who would remain in it."

As an interesting footnote, the Journal also wrote,

> Not long since laborers were digging post-holes on the premises, upon some ground where a stable had formerly stood and while at work, they unearthed the remains of an infant. This was at once connected to the apparition, but no clue was discovered by which the child could be identified, and it was quietly buried again.

The mystery continued to be unexplained and the house still unoccupied. Due to the lack of identity in the original article, it is impossible to discover whether the haunting continued, or after a hundred and fifty years someone is living on the site of this very aristocratic and mysterious ghost.

The Ghost of Henry Smith

In early August 1891, the North College area of Lawrence, Kansas, had a very peculiar ghost. Louisiana Street was believed to be haunted by a ghost standing between six and seven feet tall, dressed in black and minus a head! The appearance of this fearful ghost coincided with the death of Henry Smith, a janitor at the city clerk's office.

Appearing sometime before midnight near Smith's former residence, the ghost roamed the streets for over a half a mile. Wandering down the street with no head, the ghost would follow the superstitious folk to their doors before promptly disappearing!

Jim Walker, a young man who knew Henry Smith, told a local newspaper his story. A few nights earlier he had almost been frightened to death when the ghost had followed him to the door of his home. He was exhausted when he reached his home and fell against the door with such force that he broke the lock and literally fell into the room.

Another boy, Jim King, had a similar experience – chased from a nearby high school to his house on Louisiana Street.

With multiple sightings and newspapers regularly reporting on the activities of the ghost, a policeman called Sam James spent four nights on the street and did not witness this elusive ghost. However, on August 6th, twelve to fifteen pistol shots were heard in the neighborhood and the police could not find who had fired the shots.

Very soon, the whole community began to congregate on the streets with the hope of either seeing or capturing the ghost. Several times the ghost was witnessed, and the crowd began to take potshots at it; however, the crowd merely frightened several women instead!

As with many ghost cases of the time, it took only one person to fathom who or what was responsible. Louis Erickson explained to the Weekly Record that during the height of the ghost scare he met the ghost in black. He ran and the ghost followed him home. He could not open the door to his home and as the black figure was pressing him hard, he fired two shots at it with a revolver he had in his pocket. It was then that he discovered who was impersonating the ghost – he could see it was a boy called Will Cook who lived on nearby Warren Street. Will had dressed in a long, black garment that covered his head and had something attached resembling arms.

When the boy was enveloped in his black robe, he carried in his hands a stick by which he could raise the garment up from his head as he met his victim.

We know little about what happened next to the ghost or Will Cook. Who knows? Maybe he took notice of what the Weekly Record printed as few days later: "The Cook boy, or whoever it is, has played the game quite successfully, but it is a dangerous thing to continue, and he is likely to receive a dose of cold lead if he keeps it up."

The Giant Ghost of Benton

On Sept 13, 1896, the Philadelphia Press wrote about a fascinating case of a ghost at Benton, Indiana. Witnessed by many people from very credible jobs and positions in society, no one could provide an explanation for the strange sightings.

The Press wrote the following:

> A farmer named John W. French and his wife were the first to see this apparition. They live in the country near Benton and were driving home one night from a neighbor. The road passed an old church, moss-covered and surrounded by a graveyard, overgrown with shrubbery, and filled with the bones of hundreds who once tilled the soil in the locality.

> Ten years ago, an aged man who lived alone not far from the old church and visited the graveyard almost daily to pray over the resting place of some relative was foully murdered for the store of gold he was supposed to have hidden about his hermit abode. The robbers and murderers escaped justice, and the luckless graybeard was buried in the graveyard where he spent so much time.

> Just as French and his wife drew within sight of the white headstones in the churchyard, the horses reared back on their haunches and snorted in terror. French was alarmed and suspecting highwaymen had been scented by the horses he reached for a shotgun which lay in the bottom of the wagon for just such an emergency. But before his hand touched it he was startled by a scream from his wife. Clutching his arm, she pointed straight ahead and gasped, "Look, John, look!"

> Far down the road, just beside the glimmering monuments of the old graveyard, he saw an apparition. It was that of a man with a long white beard sweeping over his breast. The figure appeared to be eight feet in height and in one hand it carried a club, such as the brains of the old man had been beaten out

67

with ten years before. Slowly raising one arm the ghost with a majestic sweep beckoned French to come ahead. He was too startled to do anything except try to restrain the prancing horses, which were straining at the harness in attempts to break away and run. A cold sweat started out all over the body of the farmer as he realized that he was at last looking at a ghost, and then the sound of his wife's voice came to him begging him to return the way they had come and escape the doom which seemed impending. French was still too much scared and excited to control the horses, and as he gazed steadfastly at the fearful white object in the road it slowly began to move toward the wagon. The club was now raised to its shoulder, as a soldier carries a rifle, and it seemed to move forward without touching the ground, like a winged thing.

Then the farmer recovered his faculties and, whirling his team around, he lashed the horses into a run and began the trip to the house of the friend he had just left. When they arrived there both the man and his wife were almost fainting from fright.

The next man to see the ghost was Milton Moon. He had the reputation for being not only a man of intelligence but one without fear. His experience was much the same as that of the Frenches and it brought about several investigations by parties of citizens. In each case they saw and were convinced of the actual presence of the ghost without being able to discover any satisfactory explanation.

A Real-Life Daphne and Velma – Sixty Years Before!

As you may or may not know, Daphne and Velma are the two ghost-busting characters from the popular cartoon "Scooby Doo." The following story charts the adventures of two young ghost hunters in 1898 who set out to discover the ghost of Bogg's Ravine.

> For nearly a year there had been talk of a mysterious haunting on the outskirts of Rathbone, New York. The ghost haunted a hut in which in the year previously Floyd Myers had murdered Leonard Hart in a quarrel. The hut had been seized by gamblers, who made it their headquarters, when they at times spilled out to commit misdeeds. The house was shunned both on account of the murder and because criminals were said to live there. However, in 1898, the house became known for the appearance of a ghostly woman who regularly manifested to visitors.
>
> The story begins with someone named Drummer from New York who claimed that he "fell into the hands of these gamblers, who drugged, robbed him, stowed him away in a loft and left him there," printed the World newspaper. One cannot help but feel this was a lie to protect the real reason why he was at the gambler's lair – to gamble!
>
> Just after daybreak, Drummer was awakened by a curious sensation of fright; as he collected his befuddled senses, he was horrified to hear the most uncanny and heart-stopping scream of agony. The deafening silence that followed sparked his curiosity; suddenly he heard something creeping along the floor of the cabin below. He thought he had a bad nightmare until another piercing scream rang out, and then he heard the following icy words break the silence once again, "For God's sake, Floy, you have killed me!"
>
> He realized that the voice was that of a woman. He went to help her, but by the time he had stumbled down the stairs he

only saw something garbed in a black dress flit through the doorway. He rushed outside but heard and saw nothing.

Maybe it was the claims that the hut was haunted, or even somehow, they had heard of Drummer's experience, but Marie Pelfer and Katharine Phillips decided to solve the mystery.

Both were amateur photographers, and they decided to prepare a large panful of flash-light powder and take a snapshot of the ghost with their camera. It was a long and dreary vigil for the brave young women, but shortly before midnight, after having waited in a corner of the cabin since 8 o'clock, they heard the creaking of the rusty hinges of the door and saw it slowly open. To their great terror, a woman dressed in black stood in the doorway. The apparition closed the door and Miss Pelfer struck a match and in an instant the powder ignited, the flash lit up every nook and cranny of the musty old place, and Miss Phillips snapped her camera at the spook. The ghost stood for a moment with eyes glued on the young women, gave out a piercing shriek, and fled into the darkness outside.

The following day, the plucky ghost hunters spent the day developing the plate, and when the picture was finished, they were astonished to find the frightened face of Maggie Carlson, a friend of theirs who had married a woodman called Frazer.

Knowing the mystery was all but solved, they saw Mrs. Frazer that afternoon and accused her of being the "ghost." When confronted with the photograph, she confessed that she was indeed the ghost of Bogg's Ravine. Her explanation was that after her marriage she discovered her husband was a regular visitor to the gambler's hut and she had taken this novel method of frightening him and the other gamblers from meeting up. She had visited the hut several times, scared many persons inside and outside the hut, and kept her "better half" away from gambling.

The Haunted Chamber

In America as well as Europe there are several ghost stories in which the "poor man" proves his cleverness over those in power such as councilors or police chiefs. There may be an original experience attached to this story, but the likelihood is that it is little more than a folktale:

> A room in the principal inn of a country town had the reputation of being haunted. Nobody would sleep in it and it was therefore shut up, but it so happened that at an election the inn was chock full, and there was only the haunted room unoccupied. A gentleman's game keeper came to the inn exceedingly fatigued by a long journey and wanted a bed. He was informed that unless he chose to occupy the haunted room, he must seek a bed elsewhere.

> "Haunted!" exclaimed he, "stuff and nonsense, I'll sleep in it, Ghost or demon, I'll take a look at what haunts it!"

> Accordingly, after fortifying himself with a pipe and tankard, he took up his quarters in the haunted chamber, and retired to rest. He had not lain down many minutes when the bed shook under him most fearfully. He sprang out of bed, struck a light (for he had taken the precaution to place a box of lucifer matches by the bedside), and made a careful examination of the room, but could discover nothing. The courageous fellow would not return to bed but remained watching for some time. Presently, he saw the bed shake violently; the floor was firm, nothing moved but the bed. Determined, if possible, to find out the cause of this bed quake he looked in the bed, under the bed, and near the bed, and not seeing anything to account for the shaking, which every now and then seemed to seize the bed, he at last pulled it from the wall.

> Then the "murder came out." The sign board of the nut and screw came through to the back of the bed, and when the

71

wind swung the sign board to and fro, the movement was communicated to the bed, causing it to shake in the most violent manner. The game keeper, delighted at having hunted up the ghost, informed the landlord the next morning of his unearthly visitor, and was handsomely rewarded for rendering a room hitherto useless now quite serviceable.

All the ghost stories on record might no doubt have been traced to similar sources if those to whom the "ghosts" appeared had been as "plucky" as our game keeper.

This version appeared in several newspapers in 1857, at the same time "The Barber's Ghost" story also made the rounds, both of which are just modern ghost lore.

Investigation of a Haunted Church

"For several months past, a story was circulated in the streets contiguous to, and among the people living opposite, a certain church, which is not more than a mile from the old Theater in this city, that about the witching hour of night, a number of invisible spirits haunted that church," published the Washington Intelligencer, August 19 1839.

> (Ghosts) hold a kind of ambulatory conclave in the body of the building, where although no ghostly visitors had actually been seen but any of the terrified believers in the story, lights (whether blue, true or new lights, does not appear) had been noticed by a number of credible witnesses, both male and female but especially the latter, at all hours of the night, and more particularly at midnight, flitting about the church - sometimes appearing in the pews - sometimes in the aisles of the church, moving about in every direction - sometimes blazing out in awful splendor - at other times glimmering like a small taper, and casting a lurid light in the corners of the church, or suddenly vanishing in the cross aisle fronting the pulpit.

Such was the belief that the church was haunted that no person would go near the church at night for fear of witnessing the spectral happenings. The belief in the neighborhood was so strong, based on the accounts of so many respectable witnesses, that no one took the time to investigate the hauntings.

However, in August a gentleman who lived directly opposite the church was informed that the lights had been seen by not only the ladies and female servants of his family, but also by their lodger. The ladies and servants were in a clear state of distress and the lodger had to retire to his bed to forget his experience.

The gentleman accompanied by the ladies and servants stood at the door when the lights reappeared; the gentleman was astonished at what he was witnessing. He made further inquiries and discovered that the lights were always seen between 11 p.m. and midnight.

The gentleman then visited his neighbor and was able gain the keys to the haunted building for further examination:

> Procuring the keys, stationing his two friends outside, and calling in the aid of two other persons, who were casually passing through the street, to watch the side windows, through which it was suspected that the earthly intruders might have entered the church for no pious purpose; and having made all the arrangements necessary to prevent escape on the outside of the church, the third party opened the doors and entered the building, provided with a lantern and a cudgel. All the pews of the church were carefully opened and searched - the pulpit and the curtains behind the pulpit, the vestry and closet on the floor were also closely inspected, but nobody, either "celestrial or terrestrial," was there.

> All seemed quiet but then he heard gentle footsteps on the floor of the church near the pulpit; he had already checked the spot and he couldn't see anything coming toward him. The sound of the footsteps was definitely not human and slowly they came closer and closer. He began to lose his skepticism but his courage held and he open his lantern almost discovering instantly that he had a companion in the church, a large Newfoundland dog belonging to a neighbor which had followed him into the building.

> Convinced that the church wasn't haunted, the gentleman discussed the matter with his friends outside. They all believed that if the lights were not discredited then the church would continue to be known as haunted. Other alleged haunted houses in the city had caused huge mass hysteria and the gang of "ghost hunters" knew they would have to try to work out what was causing the "hauntings."

> In the midst, however, of all this consultation and consternation, it suddenly popped into the head of one of the party that, perhaps, as there was a staircase window in his

dwelling-house, which was only separated from the church by a very narrow passage, the reflection of a light carried upstairs by a member of his family might appear to persons on the opposite side of the street as a light flitting about the body of the church.

It was then unanimously agreed that the gentleman should go into his house and try the experiment with a lighted candle, when lo! it became almost instantaneously evident that the light which seemed to be flitting about the church was the reflection of the candle through the staircase window into the body of the church. Thus, the whole mystery was unraveled, and that too in the presence and sight of several by-standers who were either whole or half believers in the story of the haunted church.

It seems the cool-headed way the party investigated the church halted the reputation of the building being haunted. The incident detailed here is very similar to the circumstances of All Saints Church in Bristol, UK; for dozens of years, it was known for being haunted and, sadly, no person ever thoroughly investigated the claims. However, the "ghost" was caused by similar circumstance, a window from the neighboring house caused light to reflect into the church and give the appearance of movement from outside!

The Haunting of Clara Robertson

Brinkley Female College was a prestigious girl's school standing on what is now Fifth Street in Memphis, Tennessee. Unfortunately, the building was demolished in the early 1970s, but once it was a palatial residence that in the 1870s became a school for young ladies.

At the time of the following story, the school had more than forty students. Many had come from afar but a few who resided in the city were day attendees. It is on one of these attendees that our story is centered. Miss Clara Robertson, the daughter of Mr. Robertson, an attorney, was thirteen years old when she began to experience the paranormal.

The Waukesha Plain Dealer newspaper interviewed the Robertson family and wrote about Clara's first experience:

> Miss Clara was alone in one of the upper rooms of the institute, practicing her music lesson, when an apparition suddenly appeared before her in the shape of a girl about eight years of age, with sunken, lusterless eyes, and strikingly emaciated form and features. The object was virtually a skeleton in appearance, clad in a dingy and tattered dress of faded pink, which was partly covered with a greenish and slimy mold. It seemed also to be transparent. A sad expression rested upon the features of the strange visitor. Naturally frightened, Clara ran into an adjoining room and sprang into bed with a sick girl, at the same time motioning with her hand to the unsightly object to be gone. The apparition advanced, however, with slow and noiseless steps to the bedside, and laid an emaciated hand on the pillow, while Clara, aghast and speechless with terror, was nearly thrown into spasms, but all the time motioned away the object, which disappeared through a side door, as noiselessly as it had entered.

Clara told her teachers, parents, and school friends, only to be met with a mixture of belief, disbelief, and ridicule. He father told her that it was only a trick by some of the girls and ordered her back to school the next day. Trembling and with reluctance, Clara followed her father's instructions and returned to school; the ghost did not appear, and she began to believe it was indeed a heartless prank.

Two days later, again in the music room, the ghost reappeared. The Plain Dealer wrote that "while again practicing at the piano in the music room, two other young ladies being present, she was startled by an unusual noise, as if by some water being dashed over the floor, and on turning her head in the direction of the sound, was dismayed by the appearance of the same spectral-looking visitor of two days before. It was seen by all three, more distinctly by Clara than the others, and the trio fled in terror from the presence of the fearful apparition."

Again, the story was told to parents, teachers, and colleagues was ridiculed. However, days later, the ghost reappeared to Clara, who came running down the stairs from the music room to Miss Jackey Boone, one of the teachers at the college. Miss Boone took Clara back to the music room and, as they stood at the door, the figure of the ghost stood before them, pointing its thin finger in a southerly direction. Clara asked what it was doing there and what it wanted; the ghost replied that under a stump, fifty yards from the houses, were secreted some valuables which Clara could take possession and use to her advantage. While Miss Boone heard nothing but a rumbling noise during the conversation, a pupil present at the time heard the conversation between Clara and the ghost very clearly.

The seriousness of Miss Boone and Clara's claims that a ghost was appearing in the music room aroused suspicion that someone was playing a prank. The owners of the college, Mr. and Mrs. Meredith, undertook to investigate the matter further. The Merediths gathered all the students at the college in one of the halls while Clara was sent into the yard, the remaining scholars being questioned and examined.

Clara once again claimed she encountered the specter; she attempted to scream but the vision spoke quickly and softly saying, "Don't be alarmed, Clara, my name is Lizzie. I will not hurt you." Clara stood transfixed with terror as the ghost claimed that Brinkley College was hers by right, title, and deed, and that the present owners held it illegally having no claim to the property except her family, who were now dead. The ghost also asked Clara to obtain the deeds to prove Lizzie's claim.

The town was full of rumors and suspicion at these latest claims from Clara; many pupils at the college were terrified to return and teachers refused to work. Even Clara refused to return to Brinkley College.

Mr. Robertson decided to organize a séance and requested the attendance of a spiritual medium. Several of the Robertson neighbors were asked to witness the expected developments and were all seated around a table, placing their hands on the surface. Mr. Robertson, always skeptical and doubting the truth of the story, watched with interest in hope of detecting fraud or collusion. Within moments, Clara fainted, falling back in her chair, her eyes wide open, fixed on vacancy. Her hands began to move; soon they began to shake faster and faster and then stopped. Clara never spoke a word, but when the medium placed a pencil in her hand and paper on the table she began to write at incredible speed. At first, the characters were strange and unreadable but gradually from the scratches and scribbles a message emerged.

Questions were asked by persons present and replies were instantly written on the paper; all the time Clara did not utter a word. The account Clara wrote matched her previous encounter, that under a stump valuables were buried, five feet under the one upon which the ghost had been seen.

At the end of the séance, the medium wrote the name of the spirit as "Lizzie Davie" and kissed Clara's forehead while saying, "Good night, kiss Clara, for I love her." Clara immediately rose out of her chair and rubbed her eyes as if she had been asleep and dreaming. She claimed to know nothing of what had just happened.

The Treasure Hunt

Mr. Robertson and a party of four or five gentlemen set out later that night to Brinkley College with the determination to uncover the truth behind this ghost story and whether there were really any valuables under the tree stump. The Avalanche newspaper wrote about that night:

> Yesterday and the day before, the place was visited by thousands of persons all ages, sexes, and conditions, many of whom sought out and interviewed little Clara Robertson, the object of the alleged unearthly visitations. So great had been the rush that Mr. Meredith was compelled yesterday to solicit the aid of the police in keeping back the crowds of the curious from the college grounds, and at an early house the entrances were placed under guard, while over the main gate, in front of the building, was suspended a placard bearing in large and defiant characters, the words, "no admittance."
>
> Hundreds obtained access in the grounds, however, and gratified their curiosity, as far as practicable, in peering into the excavation and watching the diggers as they toiled patiently in search of the supposed hidden treasures, which, as revealed through spiritual agencies at the residence of Mr. Robertson on DeSoto Street, consist of several thousand dollars in coin, a quantity of jewelry, including valuable diamonds, and the title papers to the estate.
>
> Under the pale ghostly light of the moon the work of the digging for the secret began and was carried in the presence of a motley and constantly changing group, some jeering and other encouraging the work. Tom Burns, a local clerk, directed the digging and ensured that no fakery could take place. At first the diggers were disappointed to find just masonry and a partially demolished building; during the small hours the work was abandoned. It resumed the next day when the stump was finally removed, exposing more brick work and not hidden treasure.

During this time Clara was kept away from the college and the crowds; however, the ghost of Lizzie reappeared to her in the backyard of her home. Although the diggers had found nothing, the specter instructed Clara to go to the site and dig for the treasure herself. Then the specter disappeared.

Mrs. Franklin took Clara to the dig site where the diggers were still at work. Clara was urged to call upon the spirit again, which she did. Lizzie only appeared to Clara's eyes and indicated the exact position where the excavation should take place, saying at the same time that Clara herself must dig.

The Avalanche continues the story,

> Clara finally stepped into the excavation and proceeded with her little hands to ply the spade. She turned one spade full of dirt, stepped forward as if to pick something up, and felt insensible. Carried into the house she was restored, when she declared she had seen the jar, and was about to pick it up when she fell. Excitement ran higher than ever.

To cut a very long story short, Mr. Robertson requested the services of Mrs. Nourse, a medium, to communicate with the specter of Lizzie Davie, but instead her (dead) Cousin Cora answered. One can't help but feel this must have been spiritual crossed wires! Lizzie's spirit returned to the proceedings and told the ensemble that since Clara was too nervous and ill, her father Mr. Robertson was not allowed to seek the treasure. After much hesitation, the ghost allowed Robertson to dig for the treasure but said he could not open the jar for sixty days' time. Robertson agreed and was told the exact position of the treasure:

> Mr. Robertson, accompanied by the medium, and two diggers, and followed the direction of the spirit and after digging an hour or more into the brick work, found a glass jar, which he quietly passed up to the medium, whereupon they proceeded to Robertson's residence, followed by an excited crowd. The jar was at once delivered to Clara, who, regarding its possession as an end to her unearthly visitations, received it with transports of delight…. The jar bore evidence of long concealment, being covered with mold – True to the instructions from the spirit, it was not opened, but through its

sides could be seen several bags and packages, together with what appeared to be a large yellow envelope.

The editor of the Banner of Light, a newspaper dedicated to spiritualism, wrote, "The jar found is of glass, but the contents make it very heavy. Diamonds, jewelry, are to be seen, and bags which seem like moneybags. The weight indicates their contents to be gold."

Mr. Robertson informed the press and the crowds that per the instructions the jar would not be opened for sixty days' time, and he would take pleasure in giving the full benefit of watching the opening.

He hired Greenlaw Opera House for the grand reveal, charging $1 a ticket, and they sold fast. Unfortunately, a few days before the show, Robertson was attacked in his backyard. He had heard the sound of movement outside and when he went to investigate, he was set upon by four men with pistols. They threatened him with his life if he did not tell them where the jar was located; sadly, Robertson told them it was in his barn at the back of the house. The gang knocked Robertson senseless before making off with the jar. Luckily for Robertson, he was found by a servant and spent many days in the hospital recovering from his injuries.

The sightings of Lizzie continued for Clara, and she was in demand to tell her story. The Greenlaw Opera House booked Clara for regular talks and demonstrations of spiritualism; Clara's grand-sounding show was called "Holy Spirit, Angels, Devils, Prophecy, and the Gospel of Christ to This Refined Age." The climax to this show was a "demonstration of her power of the spirits"; the local newspaper reported:

> Miss Robertson seated herself near a table and went off into trance state. Questions were written on slips of paper, to which she gave incoherent answers, such as gypsies are familiar with, or such as can be seen on conversational cards – answers "that keep the word of promise to the ear but break it to the hopes." The performance closed with table-tipping.

Clara soon found her show outdated when more elaborate mediums began to tour the American theater circuit. From this point, she disappears from the media. Rumors are that up until her death many years later, Clara still loved telling Memphis locals the story of her encounters with Lizzie.

Clara's father, J. R. Robertson, decided to write a booklet called the "Brinkley Female College Ghost Story"; by all accounts, Robertson highly elaborates on the story, adding subtle details, including that Lizzie wore a pink, moldy dress during her manifestations. After the publication of the booklet, the ghost became known as "Pink Lizzie" and entered Memphis ghost lore.

And what about the haunted house itself? Regrettably, the house was pulled down in 1972, but beforehand the Historic American Buildings Survey reported on the building's structure and previous owners.

As an interesting footnote to the story, the survey discovered that historical facts did support Clara and Lizzie's claims. The house was originally built for Winston J. Davie between 1856 and 1859. In 1860 he executed a title bond to R. C. Brinkley (the owner of the building at the time of the hauntings) to secure a loan for 1,200 shares of stock in the Memphis and Charleston Railroad Company. However, because of the Civil War, the bank failed and the stock in the railway became temporarily worthless. Although the mortgage was not foreclosed by Brinkley, in 1866 Davie sold his home for an amount due to Brinkley and $15,000.

The survey continues, "The disputed point, if the ghost knew something not recorded in the deeds, seems to be the 'amount due to Brinkley.'" Had Davie repaid the borrowed stock in the now thriving railroad? Existing records are silent.

One prediction of the ghost was that if Clara Robertson did not acquire the property (via the papers in the jar) it would never be worth anything to its owner. This mild curse seems to have been enforced. Brinkley Female College closed in 1872; its principal operated Meredith Female College for three years in another location. Brinkley and subsequent owners witnessed the overcrowding and commercialization of the neighborhood, and for forty years before it was dismantled, the building was a tenement house for as many as eight families at a time.

If this ghost story was just a figment of Clara's imagination, how did she know about the Davie family and about the death of their daughter Lizzie? More importantly, how did she know the family secret – that Lizzie was buried in her favorite pink dress?

Hoffman Family Ghost

The quiet and respectable Hoffman family encountered nearly two years of hauntings and torture at the hands of malignant spirits. The mysterious pranks began in June 1869 when the family lived in Millersburg, Holmes County, Ohio. One day Mr. Hoffman lost two dollars from his wallet; at first, he did not attribute this to any supernatural entity, although subsequently he believed that it was the beginning of an ordeal that would last two years.

Mr. Hoffman began to hide his money more carefully, but wherever he placed his loose cash it would disappear. Soon Hoffman discovered that it was absolutely impossible to keep any funds about him at all. The paranormal activity increased to other items as well. Articles of food and clothing began to disappear in the same unaccountable way. Crockery fell from shelves without the aid of human hands and were smashed to pieces. Stones, eggs, and other small objects were thrown around the house and now and then showers of gravel and sand were tossed into the faces of the family. The family were naturally surprised and annoyed, but as the activity continued, they soon became alarmed. Having unsuccessfully tried every means to discover the cause of these occurrences and to put a stop to them, they left their Millersburg home.

Mr. Hoffman took another house for his wife and three children, aged 20, 17, and 15, in the city of Wooster, at some distance from their former home. Mr. Hoffman also took the step of living at the mill where he was temporarily employed in case the invisible assailant returned.

The family began to settle into their new life; Mr. Hoffman did not seem to be the target of the poltergeist any longer. In fact, it had moved its focus to Mrs. Hoffman and her children. While living on West Liberty Street in Wooster, they became victims of an extraordinary series of events. Mrs. Hoffman claimed that her clothes had disappeared and then returned in fragments, as if they had been cut and slashed to pieces. Sometimes, the garments would be found stuffed in out of the way places, such as a cellar drain or outside wood pile, or buried in earth or sand.

And then the poltergeist began to write notes to the family, sometimes appearing to be thrown from the cellar. These missives contained threats or warnings but one time the "ghost" advised Mrs. Hoffman that if she came down the stairs backwards on her knees, she would find a box containing two thousand dollars. The note gave strict instructions about the time and day when this should be done. Mrs. Hoffman, however, was afraid of bodily injury and asked her husband to perform the task. The "spirits" seemed to have known of her plan and wrote another note telling her that this task must only be performed by her, and her alone. Mrs. Hoffman refused to perform for the spirits and did not claim her promised prize.

The New York Times covered the story in May 1871 and wrote the following:

> Poundings are heard on the walls at night, stones from the size of pebbles to that of a man's fist are pitched through the doors and windows, dishes rattle, and "a general rumpus is created, as if imps were holding high revelry." A bold young man, a visitor, having said something disrespectful of the unseen agencies, a red-hot stone was dropped on his head; and on taking out his pocket handkerchief, he found it was cut into shreds.

Mr. Hoffman also began to receive "spirit notes." He decided to answer one of them and put his reply in the cellar but, just as he got upstairs, his own note dropped on the floor by his side – all his family being present.

Due to the alleged paranormal activity, mainly the thefts, the Hoffmans claimed they were impoverished, and Mrs. Hoffman and her daughter had no clothes, only those they wore on a day-to-day basis. Mr. Hoffman told the New York Times that he only had a single working suit and that all domestic utensils, plates, cups, and saucers, even table cutlery, had been destroyed or spirited away.

The New York Sun newspaper wrote about the state in which the family were living:

> Mr. Hoffman's good clothes are all gone, and what little money he has left he saves by wrapping in a handkerchief which he ties around his body underneath his shirt. It seems the spirit cannot reach that. The daughters say they have pins run into their bodies while they are asleep, and visitors have their clothes cut to pieces in broad daylight in the very presence of people who are trying to detect the cause of the disturbances.

The Hoffman's plight not only fascinated the media, but it also brought hundreds of visitors and spiritualists, all trying to communicate with the ghost.

The Fort Wayne Daily Sentinel sent a journalist to investigate the Hoffmans and wrote:

> The family...invite investigation by the hundreds who visit their house. They state that they are as much confounded at what takes place as other persons and are very anxious to be relieved of their unknown malignant enemy, who is ruining them financially, and in every manner giving them the greatest discomfort. They are afraid to sleep in separate chambers, and therefore bed in one room, frequently disturbed and frightened by unearthly noises.
>
> So many persons are constantly calling at the house that the family admit but few on account of pressure. About three hundred were refused last Sabbath. On one occasion several were declined admission because some spiritualists were at that moment deep in the mystic rites of holding a "circle," to which faith, it is said, Mrs. Hoffman is almost persuaded, having no other particular religion.

The journalist continued, providing an interesting insight into who the Hoffmans believed was haunting them, "The evil genius of her house, she sometimes is constrained to believe, is the spirit of her deceased sister, who died in Holmes County, Ohio, a few months before it began operations. Again, she imagined that it might be the ghost of her father yet thinks he wouldn't have the heart to bewitch her family."

The reporter also joined C. M. Kenton, editor of the Shreve Mirror newspaper, and two other gentlemen to visit the haunted home. The reporter wrote of his visit to Hoffman's house, "where they were shown every courtesy by the way of exhibiting piles of cut-up garments, etc., and relating the various annoyances to which the family were almost daily and nightly subjected. When about to take their departure, it was found that the reporter's hat was slashed, so to speak, into ribbons. The hat was upon a small stand in the room where all were, and could not have been moved from its place, or the action would have been observed. The cuts were clear, as if done by some lancet-kind of instrument."

Spiritualism Installed!

The Massillon Republican covered the story many times; after weeks of following the family, it printed a story about the effect of the haunting on the town, and its newspaper:

> The report of facts, published in the Republican at different times during the last six weeks, relative to the marvelous transactions of the ministering spirits haunting David Hoffman's house in Wooster, has ceased to be a local matter. Through the press it is known all over the country, until our city has rather a spiritual than truly orthodox religious reputation.

> People from distant parts of the country – from New York to Kansas, Canada, etc. have come to us for information as to the truth or falsity of the so-called Wooster spirit manifestations. Many citizens also have been verbally asked the same question.

The Republican then turned its critical eye on the visiting spiritualists and their claims:

At first the spiritualists did not know whether it was spirits or the family, but after profound research and labored investigation, success perched upon their banner. The discovery was made by a sure test – "music in the soul" – and in this melodious manner, a common tin pan, second hand, and a little wooden stick were placed under a table; the table covered with a cloth of sufficient size so as to completely envelope it; around, at a distance from a table, the circle of men and women arranged. The lights were put out, deep darkness supervened, and silence reigned so intense that one couldn't hear anybody pick up a pin. Then the stick commenced hammering the pan with a rub a-dub dub. Mrs. Hoffman and eldest daughter crowned and anointed as first-class mediums! It was glory enough for one night!

Many mediums paid visits to the Hoffman household; Madame Thompson of Cleveland was a popular spiritualist and during her visit stones were thrown across the room and the spirits made music again by banging the spoon on the pan. It was one of the largest groups of visitors the Hoffmans had experienced. Madame Thompson told the Republican that "it was spirits, but beings some many strong mediums in the Hoffman family, confusion was created, and that if she would take one of them away harmony would be restored."

And there the Wooster mystery slowly fades into history; writer Chris Woodyard claims on her website (www.hauntedohiobooks.com) that "the Hoffman family left Wooster; they went to Akron where the family seemed to shatter. Mrs. Hoffman, who had been told by some mediums that she herself had the 'Power', and her son, Jacob, lived in an apartment while Mr. Hoffman worked as a teamster and lived in a boarding house a few blocks away. Husband and wife did not divorce, but they never lived together again."

It would be all too easy to put the poltergeist down to pranks and hoaxes. Sadly, the Hoffman story is one of a family slowly being destroyed first by the death of Mrs. Hoffman's sister, then by moving to a new city, and then finally by this unusual activity. We can speculate that there may have been marriage troubles. Mr. Hoffman claimed he was sleeping at the mill due to the poltergeist, but could there have been other motives?

As with many famous poltergeist cases, the activity centered on the children; several newspapers claimed that the oldest daughter could have been responsible for hoaxing the activity, but no concrete claims were ever published. Was the poltergeist actually "real" and caused by telekinesis from the distressed children or was the oldest daughter merely looking for attention in a broken marriage?

Indiana Ghost Frenzy

From the early 1880s until the early twentieth century, the Indiana Gas Boom was a period of drilling and production of natural gas in the Trenton Gas Field that stretched from Indiana to the northwest part of Ohio. Strangely, it was during these times that there was a large increase in ghostly activity.

Within two weeks, ghosts appeared in and around the towns of Mitchell and Tipton. A headless ghost made its presence known on the old farm of Yohann Remmey on the western outskirts of Mitchell, while the ghost of a suicide appeared in the gas fields of Tipton. Soon the whole state was in an uproar and the towns began to fill with newspaper correspondents hoping to interview witnesses.

The Mitchell hauntings began when a group of boys walked through the Remmey farm and were nearly frightened to death by a ghost that allegedly rushed at them, threatened them, and vanished. One newspaper claimed that one of the boys died later, but this is unconfirmed.

For many years, the Remmey farm was known as the haunt of ghosts, and spiritual mediums. At the old farmhouse, mediums once held their nightly séances and communicated with the spirits of the invisible world. Could it be that the spirits once visiting the old building had gradually come to visit the new inhabitants?

Rumor spread that the house spirits would tell the family that one of them would become ill by knocking on the wall; the sounds became so common that the family started to pay little attention to them. However, the ghosts could make themselves known in many different ways.

One night the owner of the farm went to the door of the summer kitchen and was startled to find standing on a plank in front of the door a man with head hanging on his shoulders, blood running down on his breast, and a hatchet up lifted in his right hand. Even under scrutiny, the owner stood fast on his word, claiming he wasn't dreaming but was telling the solemn truth.

Another incident involved a hired man on the farm who also slept in the summer kitchen, but he only stayed there a short time. He complained that at midnight every night the door would suddenly open, and he could plainly see a man come and bend low over his bed.

One Sunday night, he was walking home when he was surrounded by blue, red, and yellow lights and something that looked like a flame. He rushed home at breakneck speed and the next day left for Missouri, claiming that something had haunted him every night while he slept in the summer kitchen.

Yohann's family were often awakened by the shaking of the house. One night when the boys came in late from gathering corn and lay in their hammocks, they were shaken as if by an earthquake and rattled for hours. Their chickens were in a state of shock and the farm's tools, chains, and implements could be seen swinging from their racks.

One of the strangest stories from Yohann's farm relates to when he was standing at the gate and thought he saw his daughter coming back from the spring with a bucket of water. He watched and waited for her for ten minutes but found that she had completely vanished. Upon going in the house, he discovered his daughter, and when questioned she said she hadn't visited the spring at all.

The Tipton County Ghost

In 1890, the three-times-married Alexander Yohe of Madison township, Tipton County, committed suicide by cutting his throat. He was just 50 years old, and people claimed that he had been "mentally affected" for several days beforehand.

His widow Mahala Groover was in no fit state to continue the lease of their farm, so in 1892, it was leased to the Diamond Plate Glass Company. Night and day, drilling was carried out by crews who had traveled from outside the county and did not know of Yohe's suicide.

For several nights, just before midnight, a strange form manifested near the engine; from there it would go to the derrick and mysteriously disappear.

Of course, this caused alarm among the men and the neighbors were called upon to witness the scene. To their surprise, at midnight there appeared Alexander Yohe, holding a razor in his hand and with blood streaming out of the deep ugly gash across his throat. The specter was as real as if Alexander stood there before them when living.

The ghost so frightened the night crew that the men abandoned work, and the company agreed that the drill should only operate in the day so as not to disturb the spirit of Alexander Yohe.

An Indianapolis Haunted House

In November 1860, a young man reached Indianapolis to house hunt and settle down. After several days of a weary search around the city, he was on the point of giving up. He had decided to take up quarters at the County Poor House when he noticed a For Rent sign in the window of a two-story house on the opposite side of the street. It was a house of ordinary appearance, but to him it seemed that, with its signs of age, someone was already occupying the house.

However, it became clear to him that the rooms were empty, so he made his inquiries and moved into the house in March 1860.

From that day onwards, he lived with a ghost! He often felt as if someone or something stood behind him as he walked around the house. There were certain doors in the house that no matter how well fastened opened and shut at the pleasure of an unseen power. The ghost was also witnessed walking through a bolted door!

The Indianapolis Journal published the following account:

> Members of the household have frequently felt the grasp of his ghostship and screamed for assistance. Night after night all the noise of a family household would be performed by the ghost, and the most careful search revealed nothing disturbed. Not long since the noises from midnight until 3 o'clock were all those incidents in the packing and moving of household goods. The boxes were packed with dishes and the lids nailed down and the boxes rolled out. Our gloomy friend (the house hunter) danced for joy at parting, but his happiness was of short duration for not many nights afterward the ghost moved back into his old quarters.

The house hunter never forgot his encounter at the haunted house; when journalists asked him to recollect the story they noted, "Big drops of perspiration stood upon his forehead, and he fairly trembled at the idea of being compelled to guard his family another night in the haunted house"

The Piano Maker's Ghost

In 1889, there were three very famous piano factories in New York; sadly, the New York Times correspondent doesn't mention to which factory the following ghost story belongs. I have included it for the pure quirkiness and sadness of the lead character.

In 1887, a workman in one of the biggest and best-known piano factories in this city (New York) was suddenly discharged after he had been working there for many years. He was a big fellow, weighing over three hundred pounds, and naturally his grief was large and voluminous.

He went home, thought the matter over, put a bullet in his head and died. His heart was broken.

The boys turned out, of course, and gave him an elegant funeral, and many of them were so overcome with mourning that they did not get back to work for several days.

Then the fun began.

Every night at 8 o'clock the spirit of that compiler of melody came to the factory and hovered about his old bench. It wandered through the rooms, toyed with the parts of the unfinished instruments, and filled the air with the sighs and moans and sounds of anguish. Surely, never did a sadder ghost returned to the scene of its earthly heritage.

At length it was discovered that this ghost would answer questions by the old-fashioned telegraphy of raps, and its old time friends sought to alleviate its pangs and ascertain the reason of its unrest. All sorts of questions were asked.

"Are you unhappy, dear Fritz?"
"Rat, tat, tat – yes."
"Are you sorry that you killed yourself?"
"Rat, tat, tat – yes."

There was a pathos in those doleful raps.

"Is there something you want, Fritz, very badly?"

"Oh, yes," the answer came.

What could it be? The workmen put their heads together. At length one man of genius asked,

"Is it your old place you want back? Do you want to be reinstated, Fritz?"

The reply was affirmative, followed by a whole shower of delighted raps – a tattoo of exultation.

The proprietor was summoned, and as it cost him nothing, he said that Fritz might have his old place back, and in a few moments the spirit was heard at his seat pounding away with great animation. A great load had been removed from its nebulous mind.

A Restless Spirit from Flatbush

Flatbush is one of the oldest areas of America, originally chartered as a Dutch Nieuw Nederland colony in 1651. At the time of this ghost story in 1896, Flatbush was known as "the old town"; however, two years later it became a suburb of Brooklyn and then an integral part of the larger city of New York. If you look carefully, there are still remnants of the early Dutch buildings, and maybe it was one of these that provided the following haunting.

Charles Norton lived in an allegedly early Dutch house on East Broadway near Nostrand Avenue. When Norton and his family moved into the house a few years previously, he had heard a rumor about lost treasure buried somewhere in the district.

In the early 1800s, a story told of a traveler with lots of gold in his belt who stayed overnight at the farmhouse of a Mr. Krug, a very thrifty Dutch farmer. Krug, when he heard of the large amount of gold that his visitor was carrying, gave up his own room to the stranger and insisted that he should stay there. The next day the visitor had disappeared, and when the family asked Krug about it, he told them that the man had to depart before daybreak. Strangely, the bed linens were also missing, but Krug claimed that he had burnt the bedding because the stranger had just recovered from yellow fever.

Krug couldn't keep the disappearance secret and the family discovered a man's hand behind Krug's bed. Krug had cut it off with an ax. Krug made his escape, and the family buried the hand in the basement of their farmhouse.

Mrs. Norton told the New York Times,

> Everybody who had lived here since the murder was done under this roof has had bad luck. One man who occupied the house about forty years ago left his wife and children and ran away with another man's wife; another was a burglar, and when he was caught a whole lot of silverware was found buried in the cellar; another committed suicide. We've been

here for six years now, and there has been nothing but sickness in our family. I don't like to talk about these things – it sends a chill down my back.

Charles Norton, seeking solace from the bad luck, began to excavate his cellar in search of silverware or maybe evidence of the murder – at least the ghost could be put to rest if it was buried in a graveyard. Sadly, Norton's troubles were about to begin; all he discovered were two rusty Revolutionary swords, several pieces of ancient coins, and a hand.

Could this hand be the hand of the murdered stranger? The New York Times wrote further about the incidents,

> Soon after the exhumation, Norton and the surrounding streets were haunted by a restless spirit. The ghost that walked nightly "stops at the house of Charles Norton to make inquiries for a hand that it lost there many years ago while its restless spirit was in the flesh. These visits are not fully appreciated by Norton or his wife, but it appears that Norton is to blame for the appearance of the ghost, because his ghostship was not heard of until Norton dug up the hand that had lain underground for years.

Unfortunately, we do not know whether the Nortons were able to lay to rest the spirit or whether it was a clever hoax; however, in April 1896, it was a very real ghost story.

The Return of the Union Officer

"Another spirit comes from the grave, bearing a letter in his hand to the wife of a well-known printer."
St Louis Democrat, January 29, 1867

Situated on the High Street of St. Louis, and formerly occupied by a prominent Union officer, a house with a notorious reputation once stood. In this house, the officer died and soon after a gentleman with Confederate tendencies occupied it as his principal residence. During his short stay, he was frequently awakened from his dreams by a variety of noises, raps on the front door and back door, and knocks on the ceiling as well as on his bed. The gentleman took this in stride and didn't associate the phenomena with the Union officer who had died in the very corner of the room in which he lay.

One night he was awakened by a noise like that of an owl; he jumped from the bed and struck a light. He told his wife that something was in the house and as he opened the bedroom door he heard, "Seesh! Seesh!" He slammed the door shut and it was then that he realized it could be the Union officer coming for him. After this terrifying night, the family sought other lodgings and would not discuss the incidents that took place at the haunted house.

Soon after, the editor of a "Democratic Conservative paper" moved into the house; one paper described the editor as being "fine picking for a ghost of a Union officer!" This tenant was soon to run out of the premises; a sword in the hands of the ghost – or so the story goes –so frightened him that his hair turned grey overnight. He told neighbors that he had seen the ghost, spoken to him, and was told to cease publishing scandal on Union men. Whether this is overelaboration by newspaper editors or a real account we don't know; it all sounds highly implausible.

What started out as a "simple" ghost story soon blossomed into mass hysteria with copycat appearances and anecdotes spreading across the city. One report suggested that the ghost had ventured outside the confines of the haunted house and become a neighborhood nuisance.

At a neighbor's house, the "ghost" opened the door and walked up to the owner, shook hands with him, and told him that a letter from the ghost's wife lay on the sewing machine; the ghost walked over to where the letter was, picked it up, and handed it to him saying, "give that to your wife," then vanished. There is no record of what the letter contained.

Another sighting caused quite a stir but once again, it pushes the boundaries of belief. On January 29, 1867, the Hillsdale Standard, a local newspaper wrote the following:

> We would advise all skeptics to keep an eye around, as this same ghost has been in various parts of the city. One evening last week a lady friend of ours was at the Olympic Theater, and who was well acquainted with this Union officer, saw him occupying a front seat. At first sight it sent a shudder through her, and she says she could hardly believe her eyes. When she arrived at her residence the same ghost walked out of the door as she passed in, with his hat in his hand.

As with many sightings in Victorian USA, the ghost of the Union officer disappears out of the newspapers and into the mists of time.

Was he seen again? Was it a hoax? We will never know…

In Search of a Spectral Calf

During the manhunt for Miles Ogle, a notorious counterfeiter, two agents were sent to Ohio Valley to investigate bogus coins found in circulation. The trail led to Jefferson County, Indiana, where the story of a spectral calf raised their suspicions:

> All the farmers within a dozen miles had paid the hollow a visit and waited patiently for hours to see the frisky four-legged ghost come gamboling down the hillside and go floating over the rough, rocky creek bed that was at the bottom of the hollow.

> They were never disappointed.

> Promptly at 12 o'clock the ghost made its appearance. Many carried guns and fired at the specter as it floated by. When the smoke disappeared, the ghost was gone also. This was kept up for months, and the strange apparition became quite notorious through the papers.

> The story was in this way brought to the notice of the United States secret service detectives at Cincinnati.

> They put several things together. Miles Ogle was free. Bogus coin was in circulation in the West. The ghost must certainly be a blind. The scheme was about such one as would emanate from the wily counterfeiter. Two of the detectives who made these deductions and re-enforced with firearms and ammunition started very secretly for the ghost's lair, and on the first favorable night they went to the gruesome hollow. They saw the ghost. It danced around with such surprising abandon of purpose that the two detectives were surprised. They first shot after shot at the specter but not a shot had any effect.

> The old farmer will tell you that when the two detectives came into the house shortly afterward, they were white and

breathless. That may have been due to the rough walk, and it may have not. The next morning, they made a thorough search through the hills, but could find nothing to explain the mystery.

They left the same day for Cincinnati.

Miles Ogle was later captured on a shanty-boat on the Ohio River, between Louisville and Madison, shortly after.

Miles wrote of his escapades many years later and discussed being hunted by the agents. In the book, he details some of the activities he undertook but there is no mention of a spectral calf. Was the calf really a ghost or an elaborate hoax that mystified farmers and secret service agents?

Unseen Terror of Dubuque

On February 1, 1868, the Dubuque Times published the following:

> Down on Washington Street, Dubuque, stands an old, decayed tenement house, which outlived its period of usefulness long ago but which, through the kindness of the City Fathers, is still permitted to stand as a memento of the past. A semi-decayed, gloomy old house is this, with clapboards swinging in the breeze, moss upon the roof, and many a rent in the doors and windows. Of course, a house like this would be the very place one would select as a stamping ground for ghosts and troubled spirits, whose uneasy consciences would not permit them to quietly rest where they belong.

I have uncovered many reports from the 1800s in Britain and in the United States that discuss the merits of uninhabited houses. The dark gloom of the beckoning windows and the primal curiosity is never satisfied until we explore the house's black rooms and empty corridors. It is these houses that provided the basis for many ghost stories during this era. Were they really haunted or was it local mass hysteria?

On December 20, 1867, a family from Michigan, being destitute, were compelled to live in the old house on Washington Street, Dubuque. After contacting the owner, the family took out a six-month lease on the house and paid in advance for the "privilege." The house contained four rooms on the ground floor and three bedrooms which had been abandoned and given up to the mice and rats. For this reason, the family closed the upper rooms and occupied the lower floor. The outward appearance of this rundown house may have been the source of rumors about it being haunted, but for this family it had become a home.

Just after the Christmas holidays, the husband went away from home and was detained on business overnight. On his return the next day, his wife told him about the mysterious sounds the family had heard during the night. They sounded as if someone were rolling balls across the floor and several times there were distinct knocks from different parts of the building. Her husband laughed at her experience and with assurance she took his word that the house was settling at night and that is all she had heard.

The family retired to bed as usual, but they had scarcely had the time to close their eyes when there was a rush of cold air into the room, followed by seven distinct raps on the roof above. After a short break, the silence was again broken by the apparent rolling of some heavy body in the bedrooms.

The husband sprang from his bed and ran upstairs to see what was causing the commotion. When he reached the top of the stairs, everything was quiet and how it was before. As he turned to go downstairs, he was met by another violent gust of cold air and this time it blew out his light. He called his wife for another light and began descending the stairs. Suddenly he realized that his neck was encircled by a ghostly pair of arms and a clammy hand passed over his brow several times.

The noises returned with such fury that he could hear the furniture, the chairs, seemingly being knocked violently together. The rattling of chains, broken glass, and the rolling of balls across the floor could also be heard. Sweat dripped from the man, and thoroughly frightened he made his way back downstairs to his own room where he found his wife and children in absolute terror. The husband lit a fire, and they sat all night awake, listening to the horror above them.

The next morning the man and his family packed their belongings and refused to stay another night, seeking accommodation in another part of town.

The White Mountain Ghost of Lizzie Bourne

The tragedy of Lizzie Bourne, who died while scaling Mount Washington in New Hampshire, has been written about many times. However, just twenty-six years after her death, the Decatur Democrat wrote about the night its reporters spent at Tip Top House on top of Mount Washington, in New Hampshire:

> The wind whistled mournfully around the hotel as the story was being told, and the hearers involuntarily clustered nearer one another and waited the next gloomy reminiscence. It came from an elderly gentleman who wouldn't vouch for its truthfulness, who was ready to swear that the friend who told it him was an eyewitness and could be relied upon always. The story was in relation to the death of Miss Lizzie Bourne, of Kennebunk, Me., who died in a blinding snowstorm on the Glen bridle path, on the night of September 14, 1855. The traveler, who rides up in the little railway car, has the pile of stones pointed out to him as marking the spot where her rigid body was found.

> Along with her cousin Lucy Bourne and Uncle George Bourne, Lizzie had tried to climb Mount Washington. They left the bottom of the mountain at 2:00 p.m. and at about 4:00 p.m. they had made it halfway to the top. As they walked up the carriage road, the night fell, and a snowstorm descended onto the mountainside. Quickly becoming cold and confused, Lizzie died of exposure about 10:00 p.m., her companions only just survived. In the morning when the sun rose, her uncle and cousin realized they were only a few hundred yards from Tip Top House. A year later, her family built a monument near the spot where Lizzie perished.

Reverend Larne L. Eastman was staying at the hotel attending the summit the night Lizzie died. He wrote in his diary,

Miss Lizzie Bourne, of Kennebunk Me., perished but a short distance from the Tip Top House, where we were comfortably sleeping. How painful the fact was to us; I can never describe. We were the only company present on that beautiful yet very sad morning. I helped to carry in the dead girl. After making every possible effort to revive the dear girl without success, and to comfort and make comfortable the uncle and his daughter who did but just survive the terrible night, our guide having returned, we proposed to descend. The view from the top of the mountain was glorious. The storm had thoroughly cleared the atmosphere. We could distinctly see the sun emerge from the silver bosom of the sea. Then the mighty mountains, the hills, lakes, rivers, with the milky-white clouds floating far below, here and there giving glimpses of country and village, furnished a scene transcending description….

The Decatur Democrat continued with its story:

There is a well-founded rumor that every year, on the night of the 14th of September, the ghost or spirit, or whatever you may call it, of Lizzie Bourne may be seen flitting about the mound. Henry J. Howland and a party saw it last year, and were almost frightened to death, continued the storyteller.

It was a clear, moonlight night, and Howland and his party were roaming over the summit to see whatever was to be seen. They had got down to the Bourne monument and being somewhat fatigued with their scramble over the rocks, they all dropped down for a few minutes' rest. Naturally enough the monument suggested the tragic death of the poor girl and they fell to talking about it. A heavy bank of clouds rising from the west threatened to obscure the moon altogether and give the party some trouble in finding their way back to the hotel, and they rose to start. At that moment a filmy cloud shot across the moon, and surrounding objects on the landscape lost their clearness.

105

A shriek from Howland startled everybody, and they turned to see him pointing at the monument and wringing his hands as if he was in the greatest agony. He seemed to have lost his voice after that one shriek, and there he stood horror stricken.

The whole party turned to the monument, and there if you'll believe it, continued the storyteller, glancing at his now awe-stricken listeners, was a whitish figure rising up through the stones, just as if she was coming to the surface borne upward by some mysterious stage mechanism. Then as she got to the top, she assumed a defined shape, that of a pretty girl with a sad face and flowing robes and hair.

She appeared to point her right hand toward the glimmering lights of the Tip Top House, and then suddenly dropping on her knees she clasped her hands as if in prayer. In another instant the cloud scudded away, the moon looked down as bright as ever, and the ghost or specter, or whatever you may call it, was gone.

Howland, however, was prostrated by the shock to his nerves, and didn't get over for two days. "No sir," wound up the old gentleman, "I don't believe in spirits, and I don't believe my friend untruthful. I believe there is a something or other to be seen there on the mound, and if I'm alive I'm going down on the next 14th of September to see it – alone if I can't get any of my friends to go along."

Such a story listened to with the hotel's joints creaking like a ship's and a fierce tempest in the progress outside had a marked effect upon some of the ladies, causing them to shudder and cling closer to the gentlemen.

A Séance Too Far

Mary and Elizabeth Bangs were born in Atchinson, Kansas, but their activities as mediums are more famous in the Chicago area. From childhood, the Bangs sisters performed in séances and people would pay to be entertained at the Bangs family home. Messages from the dead would appear on tablets of slate, chairs and furniture moved around the room, and children would be tied up in a "spirit cabinet" to allay any fear of fraud.

After gaining a notorious reputation that split people's opinions—messengers for the dead or absolute frauds – 1888 would be a decisive year in their fortunes. On April 2, 1888, two plainclothes officers attended a Bangs séance on the tipoff of a D. F. Tefny of Englewood.

After the usual examination of the spirit cabinet, the lights were turned down low and soon several figures alleged to be spirits made their appearance. One after another communicated with the audience and finally there appeared the spirit of a Russian princess clad in royal robes.

At an agreed-upon signal, the officers rushed forward, grabbing the "princess" and lighting the gas lamps.

The Chicago Paper described the scene as follows:

> The ghost made a furious resistance, striking out right and left, and tried to throw off the shroud and wig. "I have a warrant for you, Mary Bangs," said Detective Tyrell, and just then a light mask she wore fell off, disclosing her well-known features. A roll of something concealed under her shroud fell to the floor, and Mrs. Bangs, mother of the sisters, seized it and ran.

One of the detectives pursued her behind a curtain and discovered the roll was material probably used to make wigs and beards in the cabinet.

The Bangs sisters continued their objections to the seizure and possible arrest so much that to calm them down the officers had to draw their revolvers.

"Subsequently a search revealed a satchel filled with white muslin shrouds and the like, three sets of whiskers of different hues, five wigs, moustaches, and a great variety of make-up material, such as is used by actors," continued the Chicago Paper.

The officers also searched the cabinet and found a central curtain that made two compartments, and also a side entrance, which admitted the spirit operator behind the curtain, where all the changes of costume were made.

So, who was the mysterious complainant D. F. Trefny? Interestingly, the Bangs sisters were exposed by a spiritualist. D. F. Trefny was a Chicago-based spiritualist who complained three weeks before the arrests that the Bangs sisters' séances were frauds, and from that time onward detectives had sat in on the séances, first to expose the sisters and then to arrest them. However, it was the death of one of the sisters' major supporters that hurried the arrests.

Henry Jestram was a wealthy photographer based in Chicago. After the death of his long-term friend, August Spies, the famed Victorian anarchist who was executed for his part in a bomb attack on the police, he contacted the Bangs sisters.

Over the following months, Jestram claimed to friends that he had received on several occasions spirit communications from spies through the Bangs sisters, at whose séances he was a regular attendant.

Many newspapers of the time claimed that "his mind finally became affected by the constant brooding over the 'spirit manifestations' and a week ago it was found necessary to place him in a detention hospital for the insane." The fact that Jestram had been driven to insanity by the sisters encouraged the police to make an arrest.

The Bangs sisters were arrested for conducting entertainment without a license and obtaining money under false pretenses; sadly, Lizzie's daughter died while she was in custody. During the eulogy at her funeral, Lizzie claimed that her daughter had died due to all the negative comments and reactions to her and her sister's séances. Many newspapers of the time poured scorn over these comments.

As I said, it was a turning year for the Bangs; however, it wasn't a negative turning point, far from it. For the following thirty years or more, the Bangs sisters moved from one scheme to another – and one husband to another; one sister was married five times! They bankrupted one husband with prospects provided by the spirit world and worked with a typewriter investor G. W. N. Yost, who fell into financial ruin soon after.

They continued to apply their wares across the US, developing their act to include "spirit portraits" and writings before disappearing from public view in the early 1920s. What happened to the Bangs sisters after this time we don't know, but in their wake, they left distrust of mediums, many wrecked lives, and an enigma that continues today.

You can't help but feel that the two good-looking women used their charm and skills to outwit the upper echelons of American society.

Benjamin Stiver's Ghost Attack!

In August 1871, Montgomery County, Ohio, resident, and farmer Benjamin Stiver came under attack from a destructive poltergeist. Due to his reputation and the rumors about his farmhouse, he swore an affidavit before a magistrate that contained a detailed statement of the activity he had witnessed:

The manifestations originated in stripping crusts from pies which stood upon a shelf in the cellar. Then the milk tubs were upset, the potatoes thrown about the floor, the vinegar-barrels overturned, the chairs and tables sent flying from one end of the room to the other, the flour scattered, the chimney ornaments broken in fragments, flowerpots turned upside down, kettles of boiling water, dashed from the stove, and at last an assault was made upon the heir to the estate.

Some of Stiver's family were called upon to witness the movements of the furniture and give testimony in corroboration.

Eight members of the family appeared under oath, reciting the circumstances of the alleged poltergeist activity. The Galveston Daily News on August 4, 1871, said this about the witnesses: "The affiants are old citizens, and have the general respect of the people of that county." But does that make them "good" witnesses?

Later, Stiver became so distressed that he asked local spiritualists for an answer to his issues. They believed that a boy "medium" who had been adopted by the family was connected to the activity.

The Big Joke

During the nineteenth century, the subject of ghosts was treated with respect and pure primal fear. There are several reports in the UK and US of victims dying from the fear induced by the appearance of a ghost. Often the victim would linger for days, trembling in fear and talking riddles, or sit wide eyed and uncommunicative. The following took place in Ohio in April 1882, but I doubt such an incident would happen now in our media saturated world with computer graphics and ghost hunting TV shows.

A young Ohio man had been reading horror stories one April night and was ready to believe in ghosts and spirits. How many times have you been reading a scary book and heard a sound that spooked you?

The young man was a believer in ghosts and nightly visitors and would sleep with a revolver under his pillow in case he should encounter a night apparition. Knowing his fears, some of his friends decided to play a terrible joke on him.

One of the friends carefully drew the charges from the pistol while another dressed as the specter. They checked that their friend was fast asleep and began their prank.

The "ghost" entered the room and awoke the young man, slowly muttering and whispering. The boy sat upright, trembling with fear. The "ghost" continued to mutter and sway before the witness, but the young man drew his gun and shouted, "If you are a man, I shall kill you; if you are a ghost, this won't hurt you," and fired the weapon.

The shrouded arm of the ghost caught the "bullet" and threw it back at the shooter, hitting the headboard. He fired the remaining barrels; in every case the arm pretending to catch the bullet and throw it back at the headboard.

For a moment, the witness sat motionless as he gazed at the "ghost" and with a shriek of terror fired the last remaining cartridge and threw the pistol at the object.

With a laugh, the friend threw off the garment and into the room came his other friends, but to their horror an expression of sheer terror was on the young man's face. His mind had snapped under the strain of the terrible encounter, and he never recovered.

Death by Ghost

Several stories can be found in America's archives that relate to people being frightened to death by either hoaxes or real "ghosts." However, the following stories implicate ghosts in the deaths of individuals, but not by fright.

Charles L. Beecher of New Haven, Connecticut, committed suicide and was believed by many at the time to have been driven to death by his belief that he was haunted by his wife's ghost. On April 26, 1887, he began to prepare his end. First, he shot his pet dog and then took aim through a hand mirror and put a bullet through his head.

Charles' wife had died a few months previously and he had told neighbors that he was haunted by her spirit.

On June 28, 1858, a report about another ghost-related suicide appeared in the news. The Marksville Central Organ printed the following:

> Some two nights since, a death occurred in a certain portion of our parish, which was brought about in a strange manner.
>
> A gentleman, living unhappily with his wife, some few months since committed suicide. This so affected her that she often of a morning declared that the ghost of the deceased had haunted her during the night.
>
> Finally, one day she affirmed that the devil had appeared to her, and after upbraiding her, stated that hereafter when she should attempt to eat or drink, her food and water would choke her. And strange to say, whenever she took any nourishment, it invariably choked her. This continued for 27 days, when she died, from pure starvation.
>
> These facts we have from a gentleman of undoubted veracity.

A Civil War Ghost Story

In 1870, an old soldier shared his ghost story, which took place in "some old fields, near the edge of a dense wood that was remarkable for want of undergrowth."

The old campaigner didn't elaborate on the exact location. Although I cannot conclusively prove that "Tom Fairfax" in the story is "Thomas C. Fairfax" of the 69th Regiment, New York Militia, many of the facts and statements in the story run true to history.

It is likely that this ghost story took place at or at least near "Camp California," just outside Alexandria, Virginia. An 1866 history of the Irish Brigade wrote of the area:

> The camp commanded a splendid panoramic view of a long stretch of country. It was situated on a rising ground, near the Seminary, between two and three miles from Alexandria. At first it was covered with trees and dense brush: these being cleared away, except some shade trees, a pretty camp soon sprung up, like a canvas city. Here the three regiments were pleasantly encamped, occupying the brows of two hills, between which lies the road leading from Alexandria to Fairfax. On the right of the road, as you go from Alexandria, were the tents of the Sixty-ninth and Sixty-third, and on the left those of the Eighty-eighth. From this position there was a very fine view. A perfect amphitheater of hills girds the plains, looking picturesque with their waving forests of trees and innumerable white tents. Some rich valleys of land lie beneath, and the red brick walls of Alexandria glow in the distance. There is a slight view of the waters of the Potomac, while distinctly beyond it rise the hills of Maryland. About ten miles on the right is Mount Vernon, the home and grave of the immortal Washington.

For several nights before the witness arrived at the camp there had been reports of a strange glowing figure approaching the sentry points. Every night the soldiers on duty would report an eerie glow and figure appearing in the mist. I now leave it to the old campaigner himself to tell his incredible story:

The first night we camped there I was off duty, being ill; we were on the alert, for we knew the enemy were not far off and were expecting to see them at any moment, and our sentries were thrown out to avoid surprise. I heard the alarm during the night from the pickets, and the stir in the camp, but was too unwell to get up and see about it, as I found the alarm was not general, and the next morning laughed heartily at the tale of a ghost having driven in the pickets; but when the thing was repeated the ensuing night, I began to think someone was playing practical jokes – either the men or someone who wanted to pass the line. On the third night I was able to stand sentry myself, and Tom Fairfax and I requested the Colonel to put us on that road. He did so, and as Tom left me and went on ahead to the outer post he laughingly said – "Well, James old boy, let's find out what material the ghost is made of if it come to us to-night."

"All right; I'm with you," I replied. "If he's flesh and blood I'd not like to be in his shoes, for I don't intend he shall make a fool of me."

I forgot to mention that in the distance adjoining the field up on which we were encamped were the ruins of an old-time Virginia mansion that had evidently been built in the first settlement of the State. The main road running through the wood led past this house, but it was not on that road that the specter had been seen, but upon a by-road leading to an old mill on a rapid and deep and yet very narrow stream of water. It was a brilliant, starlight night; the moon had sunk to rest, after showing her silver crescent to the admiring gaze of those who loved to look upon nature's beauties; and the light being steady and equal, one could see for a good distance.

Fairfax was stationed near enough for me to hear his challenge, should anyone come that way. In talking the matter over, we had both arrived at the conclusion that someone was trying to pass the lines, and we were determined to catch him if possible.

As time rolled by and nothing came, I gradually ceased to think of it and my thoughts reverted to home and its loved ones, doubly dear to me, and the form of a dear little blue-eyed darling who was waiting my return with anxious, prayerful heart, was very palpable to my mind's eye; and so deeply absorbed that Tom's challenge of "Who goes there? Speak or I'll fire on you!" fell upon my ear without drawing my attention to it, ill started by the report of his gun, and, after a moment's silence, a yell so thrilling that it curdled my blood.

Looking down the road I saw running toward me on foot, to whose usual fleetness fear had added lightning speed, Tom Fairfax, the dauntless hero of a hundred hairbreadth escapes, and closely following him glided a singular looking blue light, that seemed in the distance to be a column of flame about six feet high.

As Tom reached me, he exclaimed, "Great God! James, what is it?" and fell in a dead faint at my feet.

As the thing approached me it took the resemblance of a headless man wrapped in a pale, blue flame that flickered in the night air, just looking like little tongues of fire licking the shape.

Though startled nearly out of my senses, I waited till it was within five feet of me and fired my gun right into its breast. The flame waved and opened, upon up a foot or two, and then settled back into the flickering sheet of fire, and the evil thing sped steadily past me toward the old mansion down the road.

I turned to help Tom, and as I did so, some of the guards from the main road reached us; for having heard the report of his gun and his yell, followed by my gun, they had not waited for orders, but hurried to our relief, and they saw the thing as it passed on toward the house.

We carried Tom to the camp senseless and a nice spell of brain-fever was the result of his fright, and it would take more reasoning power than I ever heard of anyone possessing to make Tom think there are not ghosts. None of the men would stay alone on that post, and a squad was left there for the rest of the night.

I was fully determined to reach the old mansion and make inquiries about it, but we moved our quarters in a hurry next day, and I never knew the secret of the headless man and that road, or what scene of crime that old mill and the ruined mansion have shared between them.

Ghosts in Times of Peace

The stories that I have collected for this first volume of 50 Real American Ghost Stories all come from between 1820 and 1899. When I started to write this book, I could not have imagined the wealth and diversity of America's ghost stories; as a ghost hunter I have been blessed!

Although I have two stories from the Civil War, both of which were reported decades afterward, I thought I would finish this book with a rather skeptical paragraph from Texas Siftings, a humor magazine from 1881:

> When stories of ghosts and haunted houses appear in the newspapers it is a sure indication that news is scarce.
>
> A haunted house is a sure card to draw attention and the reporter who fails to bring to the surface anything of a sensational character can generally fetch the public with a ghost story, well told and properly authenticated.
>
> It is a fact worth noting that no ghost stories appeared in the papers during the war. Haunted inns were closed during all that stirring period for want of patronage. Of what account would one miserable little old ghost have been when the wires were vibrating and thrilling with the stories of great battles in which men were reduced to ghosts by tens of thousands? The shocking and ghastly in real life left no place for supernatural horrors.

As they say, don't be afraid of the dead; be more afraid of the living.

References

Listed below are the newspapers that contained references or carried stories pertaining to the said ghost stories. Many Victorian British newspapers reprinted stories from United States newspapers, I have referenced the British newspapers as my source, but the chapter will show original story source.

Winslow House Hotel Ghost
Morning Herald, Thursday April 2, 1868
The Herald (Dubuque), Tuesday April 13, 1868
Austin Daily Herald, Saturday February 9, 1957

The Haunted Chamber
The Mountain Democrat, Saturday December 12, 1857

Haunted Church
Washington Intelligencer, Monday August 19, 1839 (p.1)

Death by Ghost
The Reporter & Republican, Tuesday July 13, 1858
Greensburg Standard, Friday April 29 1887

Ben Stiver's Ghost Attack
Manchester Evening News, Saturday August 26, 1871
Trewman's Exeter Flying post, Wednesday August 30, 1871 (Named as Ben Stover)

Haunted Bedstead
Hampshire Telegraph, Saturday November 9 1889 (p.9)

Ghost Clock
Hampshire Telegraph, Saturday January 21, 1899 (p.1)

A Séance too far
Reynold's Newspaper, Sunday April 22, 1888 (p.7)

Big Joke
The Northern Warder, April 11, 1882 (p.6)

Faces in the Window
The Falkirk Herald and Linlithgow Journal, Thursday May 1871 (p.7)
The Morning Post, Thursday January 4 1872 (p.8)

Hoffman Family Hauntings
Various references, mainly:
Sheffield and Rotherham Independent, Monday May 22 1871 (p.4)
Western Mail, Monday May 22 1871 (p.4)

Three Stories of Hauntings
The Manchester Evening News, Saturday May 5 1883 (p.4)

Good News for Ghosts
Shields Daily Gazette and Shipping Telegraph, Wednesday May 23 1883

Poor Bessie Brown
Various references, the main being Sunderland Daily Echo, Tuesday January 15 1901

The Jonah
The Citizen, Monday October 31 1892

Des Moines's Ghost Plague
The Grantham Journal, Saturday May 30 1874

Shooting a Ghost
The Paisley Herald and Renfrewshire Advertiser, November 30 1867

A Civil War Ghost Story
The Falkirk Herald and Linlithgow Journal, Thursday November 24 1870 (p.6)

The Ghost of Henry Smith
The Weekly Record, Lawrence, KAS. August 7 1891 (p.5)

An Indianapolis Haunted House
Burlington Weekly Hawk Eye, November 24 1860

Ghosts in the Capitol
San Antonio Daily Light, Saturday December 10, 1898
Ghosts wander the Hill - http://www.rollcall.com/issues/55_5/-36682-1.html
Albuquerque Journal, Sunday October 30 1977 (p.14)

Unseen Terror of Dubuque
Daily Gazette, Saturday February 1 1868

The Restless Spirit of Flatbush
The New York Times, Tuesday April 21 1896 (p.9)

Mrs Warfield's Haunted House
Times & Press (Fort Wayne) Wednesday September 22, 1852

Mumler's Spirit Photographs
The Bradford Observer, March 5 1863

Jonelle Lambkin rings a bell
Portland Daily Commercial, Thursday December 7 1893

Indiana Ghost Frenzy
Daily Light, Monday February 1 1892

The Live Spook
Monoquet Kosciusko Republican, February 4 1846

Piano-Maker's Ghost
Middlebury Independent, Thursday October 22 1891

Scared to Death by a Ghost
The Janesville Daily Gazette, Wednesday September 1889

In search of the Spectral Calf
The Pocahontas County Sun, Thursday March 28 1895

Return of the Union Officer
Hillsdale Standard, Tuesday January 29 1867

White Mountain Ghost of Lizzie Bourne
Various references, mainly The Decatur Democrat, October 14 1881
(p.1)

Real life Daphne and Velma
The World, Wednesday March 9 1808

The Haunting of Clara Robertson
Waukesha Plaindealer, Tuesday April 18 1871
Brinkley College Report, Historic American Buildings Survey 1972
Memphis Avalanche, February 22 1871
Memphis Commercial Appeal, July 14 1972
Brinkley Female College Ghost Story, James R Robertson (1871
Memphis Commercial Appeal, October 30 1955
The Peterburg Index, Friday April 7 1871 (p.1)

From the Author

I hope you enjoyed my first collection of original ghost experiences and the vast array of phenomena reported by the witnesses. If you would like to submit an experience or was a witness to some of the stories in this book, please email mj@mjwayland.com

For further ghost stories and research as well as my future releases please visit my website - www.mjwayland.com

Thank you

MJ Wayland

My other books include:
50 Real Ghost Stories
50 Real Ghost Stories 2
30 Real Christmas Ghost Stories
The York Ghost Walk
The Derby Ghost Walk

All are available from Amazon and other good bookshops.

About the Artist

I would like to especially thank L.E.Jeffrey for providing both inspiration to me, and incredible artwork for this book. While a good ghost story can flicker into life in our imagination, I believe the art in this book adds even more, capturing the atmosphere of a ghost experience.

You can discover more of her work at https://unseely.com/ and on social media as Unseely

Watch out for our next book together!

The Haunted Caxton Gibbet by L.E.Jeffrey

Made in the USA
Las Vegas, NV
30 September 2024